Dubois, Philip H.
    A Catskills Boyhood

DATE DUE 12/04

OCT 0 2 2006

First Edition, 1992
Published by Black Dome Press Corp.
RR1, Box 422
Hensonville, NY 12439
Tel: (518)734-6357
Fax: (518)734-5802

Library of Congress Card Catalog Number: 92-081804

ISBN 0-9628523-4-1

Cover Design by Marshall Moseley

Printed in the USA

With Special Thanks:

Patricia H. Davis

Matina Billias

Robert Gildersleeve

Catskill, NY. Collection of Michael Walsh, The Village Pub, Catskill.

Catskill, NY. Collection of Michael Walsh, The Village Pub, Catskill.

PREFACE

BETWEEN the ages of five and eighteen I lived in Catskill, N.Y. This is the story of my boyhood.

In terms of area the Village of Catskill is a small part of the Town of Catskill. A goodly proportion of the total population of the town lives in the village, which for years has numbered about 5,000 residents. My family lived about half a mile outside the village, but we shopped there, attended church there, and most of our friends and acquaintances lived there as well. And all the DuBois children attended school in the village. We lived in a rural neighborhood with rural mail service and without neighbors close by or conveniences such as city water and sewers. Our neighbors had telephones (in the early days there were two competing phone companies), but for more than a decade no electricity was available along the Athens Road on which we lived.

Since we had neither horses nor an automobile, all of us walked back and forth to the village frequently, sometimes two round trips a day. For special occasions, such as one requiring taking luggage to a boat or train, taxis became available and there was always delivery service (at first horse drawn and later by truck) for heavy items such as coal. A big load of groceries could be delivered from the village but while I lived at The Ridge, as our property was called, groceries as needed were transported chiefly by "boy power."

Our route to the village was south on the Athens Road which in the village became Spring Street which boasted a sidewalk and houses belonging to families of modest incomes. Past Hansen's Greenhouse and its outdoor growing area, we usually turned at the village cemetery corner, where Thompson Street begins. At 75 Thompson, where my grandmother lived, the street becomes quite steep, running down past Irving School which my brother and I attended, and then continuing down to Main Street, which runs more or less north and south and was the principal business district.

At the north end of Main Street, before it turns and becomes the road to Leeds and Cairo, were various businesses, including a hotel called the Smith House, a furniture store (with undertaker services available) and the plumbing shop of Hamilton Jones, father of friends of ours. Near the foot of Thompson Street were the Irving Theater that showed motion pictures, a bicycle shop, a couple of grocery stores (one of which featured an open box of fresh roasted peanuts and a hanging bunch of bananas, three for a nickel), two meat markets, and Van Gordon's store for books and stationery. Further south were a tobacco store, a shoe shine parlor and, in the YMCA building, a men's clothing store. On the west side of the street one could see a camera shop, the Nelida Theater, built for stage productions but usually showing movies, an ice cream and candy store, DuBois's Drug Store (owned by a relative), the Smith Brothers' grocery and a shoe store. On that same side of the street was Boughton's Department Store with a wonderful overhead trolley system by which sales clerks would send money and sales slips in little cylindrical containers to a central cashier and receive change and appropriate documentation in return. Offices of two of the three weekly newspapers in Catskill were along Main Street, but upstairs. After the department store came three banks: Tanners National (dating from the time when there was a tanning industry in the Catskill Mountains until the hemlock trees were used up), the Catskill Savings Bank and the Catskill National Bank, with a store in between that sold postcards and miscellaneous items. Except for the office of the *Catskill Daily Mail* with law offices above, the Main Street business district ended at the corner of Bridge Street, which went west past the Post Office, a fish market and the Armory and over the Catskill Creek to a small business district which included a yard for cemetery monuments and a shoe store. After the corner of Bridge Street and on the east side of Main Street were the Greene County Court House, the most imposing structure in town, and the Dutch Reformed Church with parsonage. Opposite were the Baptist Church and the Saulpaugh Hotel, which from the outside seemed to be a place of luxury and sophistication, but which I now suspect was, to individuals having business at the Court House and to visiting salespersons, a comfortable but unremarkable country hostelry.

From the perspective of years long after boyhood, the most noteworthy feature of Main Street was the three or four brick buildings, in different shades of red, just beyond the Saulpaugh. In early days the buildings may have been individual homes—today they contain apartments, but their collective exteriors look just like a stage setting for a magnificent opera, colorful and with interesting detail in doors and windows. This was Catskill village downtown, swarming with visitors from New York in summer, relatively quiet at other times. My brother and I went to Main Street chiefly to execute specific errands, such as having shoes repaired or to buy groceries. For a short time I was a member of the YMCA, but it had no swimming pool and the chief advantage over playing at home was a basketball court. We also went to Main Street for movies and for parades, such as took place during conventions of volunteer firemen.

Catskill is built on a sort of peninsula formed by the Hudson River and the Catskill Creek, a peninsula with a ridge rising two or three hundred feet above water level. Along the creek were a few small industrial plants, chiefly a foundry and a brick yard. The cheapest neighborhoods tended to be close to Main Street; higher up the hill housing was of better quality and the lawns were generally well manicured. A bank president owned a large white and yellow house on Spring Street with a huge lawn and picturesque pool. Along Prospect Avenue were estates with river views—said to be a favorite location for owners and captains of river boats.

Judging from residences, Catskill probably had no great numbers of either very wealthy or very poor individuals. Most property was well kept and the streets were so clean that on my first trip to New York my chief impression was of litter and dirt. All in all, Catskill was, and undoubtedly remains, a good place for growing up.

FOREWORD

IT WAS in September, 1935, that I met Philip DuBois at the University of New Mexico in Albuquerque, where we had both arrived to assume faculty duties, he as assistant professor of psychology, I as an instructor in English and assistant dean of women. I well remember him sitting across from me at a faculty table in the dining hall, tall, quiet, and with hair that was beginning to grey. We exchanged pleasantries. He was 32, I was 25; we were both unmarried and within days we discovered that we had much in common and lots to talk about.

The previous year I had been studying for my master's degree in personnel at Columbia University in New York, where three years earlier he had completed a Ph.D. in psychology. As graduate students, we had both lived in International House, and one of his professors had been Dr. Gardner Murphy, my brother-in-law. (Gardner had warned me I was throwing my life away by leaving New York for wild west New Mexico but that was before I wrote him from Albuquerque asking him what he knew about this Philip DuBois. His reply: "a very fine person." His reassurance was undoubtedly a factor in further companionship.)

Despite the Great Depression, the University of New Mexico was expanding, and very soon there were four other new appointees who joined with the two of us in expeditions to Santa Fe, Taos, Acoma and ceremonial dances in Indian pueblos. (Eventually the "sextet" was to result in three marriages, but that is getting a bit ahead in my story.) I told Philip of my family in Evanston, my undergraduate training in English and creative dramatics at Northwestern, and my personnel work at Ohio Wesleyan prior to Columbia. He was modest about his four years at Union where he joined Psi Upsilon, edited the college newspaper, conducted Sunday services in a little chapel, participated in a number of student activities and graduated with honors and a Phi Beta Kappa key. For three years he was an instructor in English at the American University of Beirut, affording him opportunity for extensive travel in Europe and the Near East as well as a return home through Iraq, Iran, Russia, Siberia, China and Japan. For the two years before migrating to New Mexico, he was the only psychologist at the Southern Branch of the University of Idaho at Pocatello.

In the summer of 1936 we were both in New York City and he invited me to go with him to visit his parents in Catskill, some 110 miles north of the city. It was there that I began to realize something of which he had not been aware: that the 13 years of the boyhood that he spent in Catskill (from 1908 until he left for college in 1921) constituted a period of significant intellectual and personal growth.

In more than 50 years of marriage, interesting details of his boyhood emerged gradually —his family, friends, outdoor activities, reading, school—all of which influenced subsequent events. It took urging on my part to induce him to spend 15 minutes a day over several months to make hand-written notes on boyhood events and then many hours translating those notes into chapters.

His descriptions reflect both the environment of beautiful woods, streams and mountains beloved by Washington Irving and the Hudson River school of painters, and the intellectual climate resulting from friends and teachers who loved books, art and music. All of this seemed to mesh perfectly with my own heritage of middle western culture with its emphasis on progressive ideas, including internationalism. The fact that my ancestors were settlers in Orange County, New York (where Philip was born and some of his ancestors had lived), may have contributed to the bond between us. But now I will let Philip's words speak.

Margaret Eloise Barclay DuBois

CONTENTS

THE BEGINNINGS

EARLY DAYS IN NEWBURGH

MY EARLIEST recollections are of Newburgh, N.Y., where I was born on July 8, 1903*. The family that emerged into consciousness consisted of parents, a brother 9 years older, a sister 7 years older and a brother 2 years younger.

We lived at 5 Liberty Street in a flat directly over the drug store (as pharmacies were called in those days) where my father was employed by the owner, his brother and my Uncle Arthur. The front entrance of the drugstore was on Renwick Street, which runs west and east down to the Hudson River. There was also an entrance on Liberty Street which runs north and south up a hill to a magnificent river view.

Directly across Liberty Street was Haight's grocery store. I don't remember being inside, but Hazel Haight was a friend of my sister Grace, and I clearly remember looking out of a window and seeing my father bringing groceries from the store, most memorably a box of breakfast cereal.

Directly across Renwick Street was a fire house, which provided excitement whenever there was an alarm and horse-drawn fire engines emerged. I never understood and never asked why smoke was coming

---

* The date deserves a footnote. The birth certificate needed for my first passport stated that "Male Dubois" was born on June 8, 1903. The reply to my query: "You were born on June 8, according to the doctor at the time of birth." When I asked my father about the error, he said, "That was just like old Doc Gleason."

Successive passports repeated the mistake until I put July 8 on an application for renewal. It was accepted without question.

out of the chimney of every engine. Years later I figured out that the mission of the fire engine was to pump water and a source of power was needed. Around the corner from the fire house and not visible from our windows was the school attended by sister Grace and Albert, my older brother who was later known as "Shorty." It was a very short walk from our home. A perfectly wonderful happening was the day Grace took me to the school for some sort of program, about which I remember two things: sharing a seat with her and pleasant attentions from her girl friends.

Further north on the left side of Liberty Street there was a soap factory of which we were made cognizant from time to time by a strong odor to which all those old enough to object made their objections verbal.

Still further north, and on the right side of the street, is a park surrounded by a fence. Inside, with a fine view of the nearby Hudson, is the historic building which General Washington used as his headquarters during the final years of the American Revolution. I remember very clearly walking on the sidewalk outside the fence and looking way, way up to my mother at whose side I was walking. I became quite familiar with the area, so I must have been allowed to play in the park—under close supervision. I really had no knowledge of the meaning of the word "headquarters"; somehow there was an implication of a head being cut into four parts.

My younger brother, formally named Henry R.DuBois, Jr., for his father, and called Harry by the family, was born December 26, 1905. Of course, I remember nothing of the occasion, even though my mother told me I could remember things that had happened before Harry was born. I do remember events when he was about two years old, especially my antics to get him to laugh as he lay in his crib. Whether I exhibited any envy or hostility, I do not know; but for years my father was very careful to show attention to me whenever he was giving attention to my brother. He developed a technique of carrying one of us under one arm and one under the other, calling Harry the "new baby" and me the "old baby." Our age differential meant that we were not playmates until he was three or four.

CHRISTMASES AND SUNDAYS

I have distinct memories of two Christmases in Newburgh, both with Christmas trees: 1906 and 1907. In the earlier Christmas I received some sort of a doll; in 1907 the most memorable present was a fire engine. On Christmas Eve Mother made doughnuts, and the tree was decorated with tinsel, strings of popcorn and balls of colored glass. Neither then nor later were gifts attributed to Santa Claus except as a pleasant fiction. "Santa Claus is a fairy," said our mother.

Sundays were special. For breakfast there were creamed potatoes and creamed codfish (made with salted codfish from a wooden box), both delicious. Other days there was breakfast cereal, Cream of Wheat, oatmeal, or a dry cereal, Force or Shredded Wheat. I also recall breakfasts involving a soft boiled egg into the yolk of which I would drop a morsel or two of white bread, a combination which I still regard as utterly delicious. Memories of meals other than breakfast are indistinct.

One meal I do remember was a picnic in Downing Park. Father came later than the rest of us and found us comfortably ensconced on a knoll. Of the menu I remember only the juicy seckel pears!

Another excursion, which may or may have not included a picnic, was to Balmville, where Grace and I gathered branches full of red berries. On the way home—perhaps to get to the trolley—we walked past a well-known landmark: the huge Balmville Tree.

To get back to Sundays, Sunday School at the Dutch Reformed Church was routine and the church seemed a long walk away. On the way we could look up at the Palatine Hotel, white and yellow and an emblem of great luxury.

One Sunday I had a traumatic experience. I had left my contribution for the collection—probably a penny—in the pocket of my reefer. When it came time to put the money in the collection, I remembered where it was and went to the wide ledge under the windows where we always put our wraps. I found my coat and felt in the pocket. The money was gone! I don't know what happened next, but when it was time to go home I retrieved my reefer and there in the pocket found my coin. I had put my hand in the pocket of another boy's reefer!

LIVING AT 5 LIBERTY STREET

Our parents had the custom of having a commercial photographer make portraits of the children from time to time. For youngsters the photographer had an iron device behind the head to hold it still. It was uncomfortable and perhaps that was the reason Albert later said, "When they have their pictures taken, DuBois children always look as though they were going to be shot!"

Next to the building in which we lived was a fenced-in yard suitable for play. There one day I found a large old-fashioned penny. In those days the yard seemed to be big, very big, but when I saw it some years later it was minuscule. Our memories of space are apparently tied to bodily movements related to that space. Just beyond the yard was the building in which Marion Blodgett lived with her parents. Marion was a playmate of my sister Grace, and became a lifelong family friend. One day I was instructed not to leave the yard, but somehow I went to the Blodgett's and was given an orange. I developed some ingenious but implausible explanations about how I got the orange without going outside the yard. Mrs. Blodgett was contacted and the truth emerged. I don't remember the punishment — but such punishments as were meted out to DuBois children tended to be just, effective and without rancor. And punishments were few. In later years my mouth was washed out with yellow laundry soap a couple of times for using bad words, and once a major infraction resulted in a light whipping.

In 1907, as undoubtedly in earlier years, there was a summer excursion to Catskill, where we stayed at the farmhouse of Aunt Hattie and Uncle Harvey. The trip was made by boat—possibly the "Mary Powell" — which my Father called the "Queen of the Hudson." I have fragmentary memories of that trip, the earliest I can recall of many happy voyages on the Hudson. I also can recall staying at the farmhouse (with no inside plumbing except a pump in the kitchen sink to draw water from a well). I also can remember walking through uncut hay over my head and running across the floor of the new house (still without walls) that Aunt Hattie was building with the money she had accumulated from many, many years of making and selling small amounts of cottage cheese.

Now back to Newburgh. By the time I was somewhat over four, I had begun social interactions outside the home. That winter a boy angered me by some sort of aggressive action, and I responded by picking up a piece of ice with the intent of throwing it at him. I was restrained and admonished. No more attempts ever to throw ice! And I made friends with Raymond, who lived up Renwick Street. I was to miss him after our coming move to Catskill.

I began to be aware of relatives. Grandmother Clough (my mother's mother) stopped in Newburgh with her husband, probably en route from New York, where they had been living, to Catskill which was to be their home once more.

THE MOVE TO CATSKILL

By early 1908 a decision had been made for our family to leave Newburgh for Catskill, where my father was to take over Aunt Hattie's and Uncle Harvey's farm and we were to live with them in their new house up on the hill some distance from the farmhouse and barn. Uncle Arthur, who owned the drugstore over which we lived, and Aunt Mame gave us a gala farewell dinner. We were to leave early in March—

the occasion may have been on February 22, because I was greatly impressed with the George Washington favors, including artificial cherries and cardboard hatchets.

Soon everything was concentrated on the big move. Mother would miss neither the gaslights nor city noises but she would miss her gas stove. I did not realize it, but I would miss Raymond and the other children of the neighborhood. Whether my father (who at that time was called "Papa" but was later called "Dad") looked forward to the move I do not know; but it would entail open-air farm work instead of indoor work as a licensed pharmacist.

Aunt Hattie and Uncle Harvey had been living in the new house for a few months and wanted the family to come. There were two important considerations: Aunt Hattie had said Uncle Harvey "was drinking himself to death" and could no longer maintain the farm; and Father's health would be improved by an outdoor occupation. Apparently a most important consideration (as I realized years later) was overlooked: the 58-acre farm was picturesque enough but lacked the fertility needed to support a family of six. Through the last third of the 19th century and the first few years of the 20th it had supported a family of two just a bit above the subsistence level. While my Father had had some experience on his father's recreational farm in Kiskatom, a few miles west of Catskill village, he was a farmer neither by training nor experience nor inclination. Mother was, however, the designated heir of Aunt Hattie, and the move was on.

The movers arrived, the flat was cleared of possessions and two big wagon loads of household goods were on their way to the freight station. Trunks were packed, everyone bundled up for the March weather and soon we were all down at the railroad station where, at Albert's pointing, I watched the trunks being slid down an incline from one level to another.

It was probably my first train ride, since summer travel was always by boat: cheaper and more enjoyable. I loved looking out of the window. Baby Harry at two years of age must have taken most of the attention of Grace and our parents. Albert, almost 14, had his own money and showed his independence by buying a bar of chocolate from the "butcher." One of the techniques of a train salesboy was to put a candy bar on everybody's seat arm, and collect from those who accepted it. I was under strict instructions not to touch—hence my awe of a brother who could do as he pleased and who gave me part of his bar.

Uncle Harvey met us at the station and soon, in the horse-drawn carriage that the two older children called the "band wagon," we were at our new home. A few days later a procession of three wagons brought our furniture.

OUR HOME IN CATSKILL

The new house was called "The Maples," from the surrounding ring of trees which had been planted many years before in anticipation of building. In the early stages they had been kept alive with pails of water carried by hand from the farmhouse a quarter of a mile away. Since several boarding houses in Greene County were called "The Maples," Father eventually decided the place should be called "The Ridge," a name it retains. Grace and Albert were soon busy with school, but since winter was not quite finished I saw them sledding on a patch of snow in a field across the valley to the east.

It didn't take me long to decide that I didn't like Catskill. The village was half a mile away and I had no playmates: Raymond, of course, was back in Newburgh; Harry was only a few months over two and Grace and Albert were too old. Years later my mother told me that I was good at finding things to do and at amusing myself. If so, it all started in those boring two years between arriving in Catskill and starting grade school.

The summer of 1908 was not too bad—Father was doing farm work and I sometimes could ride the lumber wagon into the fields. Once, while he was closing a gate through which we had just passed, the team ran away with me sitting on the flat bed of the wagon. I was scared, but I held tight and the team stopped quietly at the next gate. Occasionally I was taken to the barn at milking time; and once I ran there all by myself, much to Mother's alarm. I was warned not to run away again. I don't think I ever did.

Father continued Uncle Harvey's milk route in town—at least he ordered two crates of H.R.DuBois milk bottles from the Corning Glass Works. The milk route was discontinued before the bottles could be put in service and the crates, placed in the attic at The Ridge, remained there for years and years.

The attempt to farm was disastrous financially to Father who had to use accumulated savings, and in the summer of 1909 he found a job as a druggist on Long Island. While he was away I came down with what Dr. Vincent diagnosed as typhoid fever. Maybe it was—Dr. Vincent pointed to some red spots—but the fever lasted for only a few days. I remember most vividly being fed "egg nog," consisting of a mixture of milk and raw egg and administered through a feeder. I have avoided anything resembling egg nog ever since. Much pleasanter were the roses that were brought from the garden, and a calico cat that purred and purred. Dr. Vincent always arrived in a horse and buggy driven by a friendly black man, Frank Hasbrook. And I had a kind nurse who sent me a postcard after I recovered.

SCHOOL DAYS

I was six in 1909, normal age for entering school, but the decision was made that I was not to enter school until the following year. I continued to be bored despite the friends my older siblings brought to The Ridge. By this time Harry was walking about and I must have interacted with him, but a chief occupation was copying letters and numerals and asking their names. I still make my 5's and 6's in my self-taught fashion of starting at the bottom. Before going to school I could not read—but I knew the alphabet and I could count to 100. I knew that a difficult task awaited me in school, learning how to write "in connected letters." And I knew that in many ways school would be a big change.

In 1910 the house in which we lived was in a rural school district with a one-room school half a mile up the road. However, it was decided that I should attend the grade school in the village of Catskill even though there would be tuition to pay. (A year or so later the rural district was incorporated into the village school district and no further tuition payments were needed.) So one morning my mother took me to the first grade in the Irving Elementary School, three quarters of a mile from our home and which I had remembered seeing under construction in 1907. A very kindly Miss Hale received me in a room filled with youngsters, apparently too many for a single classroom, so with a number of others I was taken to Miss Slattery's room in which there were both the overflow group of first graders and a similar group of third graders, a situation which turned out to be something of an advantage. Since I already knew the alphabet, reading in the primer was absurdly simple, and from time to time I listened to what the third graders were doing. Probably that contributed to an unexpected turn of events in June—I was promoted to the third grade, skipping the second. This led to some teasing by Shorty's friends. Since I had not attended kindergarten the year before first grade, I was now accused of being in "skiptagarten."

When I was in first grade a friendly janitor sharpened our pencils with a knife as we stood around during recess awaiting our turn. A year later, a new invention—a pencil sharpener operated by a crank—was introduced and we could sharpen our own.

The lunch recess was an hour and a half, during which I usually walked home. In stormy weather I had money to buy a can of Campbell's vegetable soup and take it to my grandmother's, only a block or so away. She would heat the soup, and provide a cup of Postum and a wonderful molasses cookie. In later years and through high school, Grandmother's house was a safe and convenient place for Harry and me to leave our bicycles.

Mother was somewhat over-protective of me, and I was under strict instructions not to play in the school yard. "The big boys are too rough," she said. This restriction did not apply to Harry two years later and he was quite skillful in making friends. In the third grade I encountered Edward Jones who lived in one of the first houses in the village on my route to school. Edward and I became lifelong friends.

There was continuity in the six years in the Irving School. Nine months of classes alternated with three months of summer vacation. Nothing was stressful in either the academic or social situation. The teachers—all unmarried women—were competent and supportive. Miss Putnam, my third grade teacher, later married Dick Kennedy, a teller in the Catskill Savings Bank, where in 1912 my mother started an account in my name with pennies from my piggy bank. I still have the account.

Miss Hull in the fourth grade was older and motherly. She was patient and helpful when I made mistakes in long division. "You're just not treating the numbers right," she said. Had Miss Hull in later years read some of my papers on quantitative methods in psychology she would have been pleased with my progress in learning "how to treat numbers right."

World War I began the summer before I entered fifth grade. I had read in a Sunday supplement about the invention of mechanical soldiers who would be shooting each other in any future war, so at first I thought the war would be bloodless! What fantastic junk is sometimes published!

LATER GRADES

In Miss Stone's fifth grade I was involved in a problem. We had a physiology class in which there was a description of amputation. I felt very, very queer; walked to the front of the class; said I was going blind; and fainted. I came to in the teachers' lounge room. A doctor came who administered whiskey which tasted so bad that I spit it out. At home the routine was careful care for two or three weeks, and, since there were no further symptoms, back to school, where I was excused from further physiology lessons. Sixty years later the trouble was diagnosed. When I complained to my physician of occasional giddiness, he proved to me that it was just a matter of overbreathing, which I tended to do in stressful situations.

One year while I was in grade school it was decided that I needed to have an operation to remove tonsils and adenoids. Mother took me to the local hospital, situated in West Catskill. Dr.Hungerford, then our family physician, was the surgeon, Dr.Rapp; the anesthetist. The administration of the ether was traumatic—I still remember my images as I went under—and I was very sick as I came out. Everything, however, went according to plan, and I was ready to go home after one night in the hospital.

Miss Wheeler in the sixth grade was quiet, firm and effective; and in the seventh grade the teacher was Miss Lewis. She had difficulty in pronouncing the word "geography," but, as with all my other teachers, maintained an orderly classroom and a program geared to student learning. Pupils were expected to learn and did so within their limitations.

My poorest subjects in grade school were penmanship and spelling, and I didn't like the music lessons taught by a special teacher who trained us on reading do-re-me's from staves and skipped all the songs with words. Somehow in the later grades and in high school we did a lot of singing, and in following years, as I became familiar with arias from operas and the works of Gilbert and Sullivan, I was surprised at my familiarity with them that dated back to school days. I don't remember any training in the visual arts. However in one grade, the sixth I think, the girls were being excused from regular lessons to go over to the high school building for "domestic science," that is to say, cooking. Some of us objected to the discrimination. The principal of the Irving School, who was also superintendent of the Catskill schools, agreed with us and we had a number of informative cooking lessons with high school equipment, culminating in an early morning class-prepared breakfast. For some reason boys in following classes did not have this constructive experience.

OUTSIDE READING

Instruction at the Irving School was competent but strictly within the New York State guidelines. I cannot remember a summer reading list or even any suggestion that it would be a good idea to read books outside of class. But we did read: books about war, boys traveling in far places, high-tech adventures. Many came from Appleton's book factory in endless series, including the Rover Boys and the Motion Picture Boys. Since Appleton's books carried the names of different authors, we debated their relative merits. Dozens of Horatio Alger books were available—new reprints at 10 cents each and all with much the same plot. A poor boy works hard, makes ethical decisions, and achieves final success with the help of a benefactor. The Appleton books were less accessible since they cost 50 cents a piece but sometimes could be borrowed from friends. In our attic I found several Henty books, always about war and written as I found out later by an English army officer. "The Franc-Tireurs of Dijon" introduced me to the Franco-Prussian War of 1870, and I think Henty was the author of a book about the adventures of a young northerner serving on a gun boat on the Mississippi River in the American Civil War.

As Christmas presents I received books about young men in the American Revolution written by Henry T.Tomlinson, whom Dad identified as one of his teachers at Rutgers Prep. These were a cut above the Alger and Appleton books in style and plausibility. When boys' books ran out there was an occasional girls' book as well as adult novels: "The Girl of the Limberlost," "Freckles," and "The Purple Stockings," which, at the age I attempted them, were far from absorbing.

THE RIDGE AND ITS PEOPLE

Aunt Hattie was Mother's aunt. Mother's mother, Juliet Clough, married Franklin Clough in the 1860's. He died quite young (when Mother was two), and after a time she married Albert Clough, who fathered Aunt Milly. Franklin Clough had left his wife with two small girls, my Aunt Ella and Mother. Apparently two children were too much of a burden and Aunt Hattie (who was childless) agreed to raise my mother. Mother's felt obligation to Aunt Hattie in her old age was one of the reasons why the DuBois family moved from Newburgh to Catskill.

The Browns (Aunt Hattie and Uncle Harvey) moved into the new house after its completion in 1907. The six DuBoises arrived in March 1908. For a year or so eight of us lived in the four bedrooms. The Browns had the only heated bedroom. It had bay windows with southern exposure. Another large bedroom, with a south window and two windows on the west opening on a balcony, was occupied by my parents and by the two year old in his crib. Grace had the room at the northwest, Shorty the room at the northeast, both with two windows. Until I was ill in the summer of 1909 when I had temporary quarters in a larger room, I slept on a cot, probably in Grace's room.

After Dad's summer work on Long Island in 1909, he bought Lape's drugstore in Athens, four miles north of The Ridge, which became the chief source of family income for several years. He came home every Sunday, sometimes walking, sometimes coming on the "Isabella" or the "Robert Livingston," getting off the boat at an icehouse dock. When Shorty left for college in the fall of 1913 I inherited his bedroom, which became mine for eight years. Grace left for New York in

1917, so from then on Harry had a room of his own. Uncle Harvey died in 1919 and Aunt Hattie in 1923, with title to the house and the farm going to Mother.

While World War I was raging in Europe, Uncle Arthur wanted to retire from business, so Dad sold his Athens store and bought Uncle Arthur's. For 9 or 10 years Dad lived in a boarding house in Newburgh, coming up to Catskill for a few days each month. The store was far more profitable than the one in Athens and he would have liked to continue with it for a few more years, but after all the children were scattered and Mother was living alone at The Ridge (having refused to move back to Newburgh even temporarily), Dad sold his store and retired. For years they were congenial companions, with frequent visits from their children and assorted family members. Dad kept up his pharmacist's license and from time to time worked at a drugstore in Catskill. Occasionally he had a longer assignment out of town.

LIFE AT THE RIDGE

At The Ridge we were living "in the country," and it never occurred to me that we had deprivation of any kind. Our advantages were obvious: woods and hills for play, quiet days and nights, beautiful views, especially a view of the entire Catskill range, eight miles or so away at the nearest point. Our village friends had unlimited running water, lights that would go on and off at the flick of a switch, and telephones. All our water was channeled from our roof to a cistern, and for house use had to be pumped by hand with a long lever to a tank in the attic. We did have an upstairs bathroom, but because water was not plentiful and required labor to get it into the tank, we all used an outdoor facility as much as possible. Our bathroom had a tub but no shower. An inside bathroom was such a luxury in country houses that Aunt Hattie, who wrote frequently for publication, successfully submitted an article on the subject to the Farm Journal. It was entitled "Better Than a Parlor." When the cistern ran dry, usually in the summer, it was up to the boys to clean it. We would climb down on a ladder, taking pail and mop and anything else we needed to scoop up all dirt and decayed leaves carried down from the roof. All this had imparted a peculiar taste to the water, to which we were well accustomed. (The village water was not considered much safer—at that time it was pumped from the Hudson River with little purification.) We had skilled help when a leak was discovered in the cement bottom and when new lead-in pipes were needed. When the cistern was dry we carried water for drinking and cooking from a well on Kerr's property across the road. Years later when Harry took over the property, he had a fine artesian well drilled, with

appropriate pump and tank, so that now there is no water problem at
The Ridge.

To avoid the confusion that could develop with two families
living in the same house, it was made clear that orders for the boys to do
chores were to come only from a DuBois parent. The Browns did their
own gardening—a separate tract was assigned for DuBois lettuce, rad-
ishes, peas, beans, beets, cauliflower, corn, potatoes, carrots and tomatoes. Harry and I worked in the garden with somewhat limited enthusiasm. While the flock of chickens was basically a Brown enterprise,
DuBois boys were often required to feed the chickens, to gather eggs, to
break up oyster shells to insure strong egg shells, to deliver to customers
eggs which Aunt Hattie had available for sale, and the not very pleasant
task of cleaning the hen house. We also gathered the manure for use as
fertilizer.

The flock supplied not only eggs for regular use but chicken for
the Sunday dinners, joint affairs of the two families. As soon as I was
mature enough I was given the Saturday assignment of decapitating the
chicken with an axe, dunking it in a pail of almost boiling water,
plucking the feathers and removing the entrails.

Some of our food, coming from our own fruit trees, required
processing. Out front there was a crabapple tree, yielding ingredients
for delicious jelly. Another jelly was made with the quinces from a tree
at the foot of the garden. An Astrakhan apple tree yielded fruit very
early in the season, good for a snack but rather poor for household
purposes. Plums were abundant and better: small blue plums for jam
and large green plums for eating out of hand. However, after some
years, the trees of both varieties were damaged and then killed by a
blight.

There were a couple of "half wild" cherry trees not far from the
house. The fruit was never as large nor as sweet as cultivated cherries
nor as small and puckery as wild cherries but had a pleasant taste. Harry
and I (and occasionally a friend) would be in one of the trees half an
hour at a time just eating cherries. Aunt Hattie wanted us to bring some
to the house for cooking but somehow we never got around to it.

VESTIGES

Prior to the advent of Europeans in the Hudson Valley the region
had, of course, been populated by Indians. However, when I was growing up in Catskill few vestiges of the Indians remained. Once our
neighbor, Becky Hallenbeck, picked up an arrowhead from between a
couple of rocks and other finds of arrowheads were occasionally reported, but no pottery or tools.

The Dutch settlers who came to the valley after Henry Hudson's voyage up the river in 1609 left in the Catskill area numerous descendants, a flourishing church, many Dutch place-names, a few language remnants, and some quaint stone houses.

The Huguenots from whom I received my French name at first married within their own group but soon were drawn into the surrounding Dutch peoples to the extent that they spoke Dutch, kept records in Dutch and became members of the Dutch Reformed Church. My father's mother was a Wyncoop and his father, Anson DuBois, had more than a little Dutch blood in his ancestry.

My mother was three-quarters of Dutch descent, and proud of it! In her mother's childhood in the 1840's, the children were forbidden to speak Dutch while the parents spoke Dutch when they did not want the children to understand. But the children did understand and even remembered a bit of the language into adulthood. At good-night time at The Ridge we often were wished "Schlaven-sie voll!" and Aunt Hattie could recite the nursery rhyme which begins "Trippe! troppe! trontje!"

Many place names in the Hudson Valley owe their origin to the Dutch: Strake, Plaatje, Saugerties, Coxsackie, and all the streams with "kill" as part of the designation: Catskill, Kaaterskill, Vosenkill. And then there is the word "clove" applied to deep clefts in the mountains: Palenville Clove, Kaaterskill Clove, Plattekill Clove. I did not realize that the word so used was not English until no one understood me when I used it one day in college. And of course a fair percentage of the families living around Catskill have Dutch names: Overbaugh, Becker, Van Gordon, Hallenbeck, Van Orden, Van Ness and Vedder. Perhaps the best known surviving specimen of Dutch colonial architecture is the Bronck House in Coxsackie. But Catskill has three Dutch stone houses, the Van Vechten House and two houses built by members of the DuBois family.

The Dutch Reformed Church continues to be strong in the Hudson Valley, constituting a living vestige of the days when settlers from the Netherlands came to establish farms in one of the most beautiful areas of the New World.

PEOPLE AT THE RIDGE

AUNT HATTIE

IN 1908-09 I was becoming more and more aware of the Browns, my parents, my sister and my two brothers. Of the two Browns, Aunt Hattie had the wider interests. Her mother, whose maiden name was Wells, was of English extraction, the rest of her ancestry being Hudson River Dutch. The Dutch name was originally Klau, a name which appears in rosters of local Revolutionary War militia, but which her branch of the family spelled Clough, and other branches spelled Clow or Clowe. Born in 1844, she was not too far removed from the American Revolution, in which the Dutch farmers of the Hudson Valley had no use for the English. When she was a child an older relative who had lived in revolutionary times vehemently denounced the "Tories," and she herself had unkind things to say about her English relatives.

Aunt Hattie certainly went to school—for how long I don't know—but she talked grammatically and wrote clearly. Her numerous articles for *The Farm Journal* were accepted with little editing. After her early marriage to Harvey Brown, Aunt Hattie worked hard on his farm. In connection with his purchase of additional land, she lent him some money for which she received a note. Neither interest nor principal was paid, and eventually the note was the basis of her acquiring title to the farm just before Uncle Harvey died. He didn't like the idea of signing the paper validating the note, but eventually he acquiesced, and, since he had no will, legal procedures on his death were simplified.

When, somewhat before our move to Catskill, she became disturbed about her husband's drinking, she became an enthusiastic member of WCTU, the Women's Christian Temperance Union, attending chapter meetings and writing occasional articles for its publication, *The*

Union Signal, which came to the house regularly. Her cause was prohibition, and all progress toward it was followed carefully. When it seemed that males were thwarting the drive toward prohibition, women's suffrage seemed a likely facilitating step, so she became an early and energetic advocate of "votes for women." To get a bit ahead of the story, at her death in 1923 two amendments to the U.S.Constitution had been passed: prohibition and votes for women. As difficulties with prohibition had not yet become obvious, and as women's suffrage still seemed the key to reform, her years of advocacy seemed to have been rewarded.

Aunt Hattie was an enthusiastic grower of flowers. She was not a gardener in the sense of a person who is concerned with a garden aesthetically arranged as a place for leisurely enjoyment. Dahlias were her specialty and they were planted in hills like potatoes. At one time she had 60 varieties, mostly ordered by mail from various suppliers. The clay soil of The Ridge seemed to have been excellent for dahlias, especially when supplemented with chicken manure for which the family name was "henminey."

Other flowers she raised one or two plants at a time, with a view of competing for prizes at the Greene County Fair, held annually at Cairo a dozen miles away. At fair time she would hire a car to go to the fair both to participate in a WCTU publicity effort and to exhibit dozens of different plants—and the prizes more than paid her own immediate expenses. Her chief rival was Florence Cole Vincent, a granddaughter of Thomas Cole, the painter, and occupant of his former home as well as the wife of our family physician, Dr.Vincent. The friendly competition went on more or less evenly for years.

The DuBois and Brown families used the same kitchen with a stove burning either wood or coal—but the Browns ate in a kitchen alcove while the DuBoises ate in the dining room. On special occasions, always including Sunday noon as mentioned earlier, the families ate together. Once in a while we youngsters did get a taste of Aunt Hattie's delicious creamed potatoes, of which Mother disapproved because they contained a liberal amount of pepper.

Parts of Aunt Hattie's costumes from her early days were in the attic, including a bustle which, she once remarked, she and her girl-friends of Civil War Days wore with special pleasure. When she dressed for church or for a meeting in town she made an excellent appearance but around The Ridge she dressed chiefly for work—and work she did. She seemed very strong and didn't shy from wielding a shovel or a pickaxe. Her sister, Grandmother Clough, seemed frail by comparison—yet Aunt Hattie died in her seventies while her sister lived to be ninety.

Aunt Hattie took her stewardship of the niece who became my

Mother very seriously. She saw to it that Mother graduated from the Catskill Free Academy (now Catskill High School), an uncommon achievement for farm children in 1888. Mother also had music lessons, with practice on a melodeon which later became a decorative but non-functional piece of furniture at The Ridge.

When not busy with work, Aunt Hattie read avidly, mostly her magazines and *The Catskill Recorder*, a weekly local newspaper, and *The Knickerbocker Press*, a daily paper published in Albany 35 miles away. She sometimes consulted *The Farm Almanac*, and, from time to time, her Bible, even though she disapproved of Saint Paul's permissiveness in the matter of wine.

UNCLE HARVEY

The Uncle Harvey I knew was pretty well dominated by his wife. He was certainly easy-going and probably friendly with his peers. He made no out-going gestures to the children who came to live in his home, and who on very rare occasions and contrary to instructions indulged in unfriendly capers toward him, such as ruining some grafts he had put on a wild pear tree. I remember only one time when he had something to drink at The Ridge. He smuggled a bottle into the cellar and spent much of the day going up and down the basement stairs for a nip.

Smoking was a different matter. He bought chewing tobacco, and after it was chewed, dried it in the sun and then smoked it. All this was permitted by his wife—but his use of tobacco was restricted to outdoors and, in inclement weather, to the cellar, where he had a comfortable chair right next to the furnace. He worked at growing vegetables but Aunt Hattie was vociferously annoyed when he disappeared into the garden just as she was about to announce lunch. Once in a while Harry or I would have a quiet chat with him in his below-ground retreat. He was certainly not lacking in intelligence but his interests were limited.

DAD

The last time my father, Henry R. DuBois, lived full-time with his complete family was the year he attempted to be a farmer, 1908-09, when he was 40 years of age. He sometimes described himself as the third son of the third wife. His father, Anson DuBois, belonged to the fifth generation of a Catskill family of French Huguenot extraction and achieved distinction as a minister of the Dutch Reformed Church, which was embraced by the Huguenots as they became a small minority in their Dutch-speaking communities. Rev. Anson DuBois, a graduate of

Rutgers College and Rutgers Theological Seminary and with a D.D. from Union College, lost two wives in childbirth before marrying Dad's mother, the daughter of another Dutch Reformed pastor, Rev. Peter Wyncoop. Dad's appraisal of his father: "a good man but his sermons were very dull."

When his parents went to the Danish West Indies (now the Virgin Islands) on a missionary assignment, Dad was left behind as a boarding student at Rutgers Preparatory School. It was a situation he didn't like. Instead of college, he attended and graduated from the New York School of Pharmacy, which eventually became a part of Columbia University.

Dad and Mother had a warm relationship that endured much separation brought about by Dad's working first in Athens and later in Newburgh. If there were disagreements, they were behind closed doors. Fifteen years of seeing each other only on Sundays or for a few days each month were followed by eighteen years in which they were reunited full time at The Ridge. Although Dad in his retirement was under-employed, these years were, I think, basically very happy.

But to get back to Dad as a father. After 1909 full time parenting was left to Mother, but Dad gave generously of his time whenever it was available. He could be playful. When I was about five he persuaded me to attempt to bring him a spot of sunlight at the end of a sunbeam in the room, a task which turned out to be educational. On another occasion he demonstrated how he could eat a candle. What he brought into the room certainly looked like a candle. He lit the wick, blew out the flame and then consumed the "candle," which he finally revealed as a piece of apple cut with a corer and with a bit of almond as the "wick."

He was a good person to talk with about important decisions, such as whether to buy a copy of the first United States postage stamp for my collection. (He supported the idea and I still have the stamp.)

He left sex education to Mother and to chance. When he was farming the two of us took a cow to a neighbor's farm "to see the bull," but at what I later knew was the crucial time I was instructed to run behind the barn and stay there until called. There was talk from time to time of cows and bulls and I confessed that I could not tell the difference. My father's response: "When you're old enough, you'll know a sure way of telling the difference." I have no recollection of just when that time arrived.

He always loved history and was annoyed that his parents had saved him no newspapers from Civil War days. Conan Doyle wrote a history of World War I and during the war Dad bought the volumes as they appeared. He was a devoted reader of a more memorable Conan

Doyle enterprise, the Sherlock Holmes stories. In his retirement he read many books and I remember he wanted me to interpret some of the French phrases in *Vanity Fair*.

By the summer of 1941 Dad was in his last illness and our little family of three visited The Ridge to see him. His nurse was making him fairly comfortable but he could surmise the prognosis only from his increasing enfeeblement. I saw him looking out of the window as we drove away. He died a few months later when I was in military service in World War II.

OLDER BROTHER "SHORTY"

Of the four DuBois children who survived infancy, Albert, often called "Shorty," was the oldest, physically the largest (six feet four), and, at least in Mother's evaluation, the most headstrong. The other children were much easier to handle, perhaps because when they came along she was more experienced. I don't know when he acquired his obviously antithetic nickname—probably in high school—but except for his mother, who always called him Albert, he was Shorty to all who knew him. He was a natural athlete, fast and powerful. Beginning in high school, he excelled at football and was good in other sports. In addition to winning a football letter each year he was in college, he won another letter for throwing the discus.

He was born July 21, 1894, exactly nine months and three days after his parents were married. When at the age of eleven he was shown the second of his baby brothers, he is reported to have said, "He's all right, but we don't want too many of them running around." He enjoyed dominance—and perhaps one reason why I became a good student and eventually had an intellectual career was that I discovered an area where I could compete with an ascendant older brother.

Shorty spent five years graduating from Catskill High School. Mother said he spent much too much time in his love affair with Margarite Craigie, daughter of the publisher of *The Examiner*, a local newspaper. Margarite was a beautiful and lovely person, who wisely decided not to wait years for Shorty but to marry a ready and willing Episcopalian rector. The decision led her to cry all night, she said, but her marriage was happy.

Paying Shorty's expenses at Union College, which he entered in the fall of 1913, must have been quite an undertaking for Dad and Mother. He entered in engineering but majored in football and his fraternity, Psi Upsilon. He "busted out," transferred to the University of Ohio on a football scholarship and, with his teammates, volunteered for military service soon after the United States entered World War I in

April, 1917. After training at Fort Benjamin Harrison, he was commissioned a second lieutenant and sent to France for training as a field artillery officer. He was assigned to a combat unit in the Rainbow Division and soon saw action. His experiences in over a year of combat were so horrible that for years after his return he would say practically nothing about them. Later he told of a few happenings. It seems that an American infantry commander was contemplating an attack on a hill occupied by the enemy. The commander refused artillery help by way of a preliminary bombardment, saying, "We want to go up and surprise the Germans." The result: a hill covered with dead American soldiers.

Another story involved a bombardment during which his outfit took refuge in a dugout. Then Shorty remembered a case of beer he had stashed somewhere outside. "Wine," he said later, "was plentiful but good beer was scarce." Despite explosions of enemy shells, he left the dugout, rescued the case of beer and brought it back, to an angry tongue-lashing from his commanding officer. "If it had been a man," Shorty said, "my chest would have had a string of medals!"

Shorty was gassed and out of action for a time, and he saw so much bloodshed that he expected to die in France. But he survived, was on the Rhine with the occupation forces for a few months, and, as a first lieutenant, returned to The Ridge in the middle of the night, calling out to Mother, "Your oldest son has come home to die!" He worked as a manual laborer for a few months and in the fall of 1919 went back to Union College with the educational support awarded to veterans. Academic success eluded him again and in the spring semester he concentrated on winning a beautiful white sweater with a garnet "U" to give to Dorothy, a lovely new girl friend at Skidmore, a nearby college for women. It turned out, however, that Dorothy's plan for her future did not include Shorty.

He worked at different jobs in the New York area, and finally met and married Evelyn Morrisey, attractive and capable, with whom he shared life and fortune for more than half a century. After Shorty became manager of a large Sears Roebuck store in Westchester County they bought a fine home in Bronxville. Shorty took time to become involved with community affairs, including serving on a youth-centered board. When not busy with her responsible position in the disbursement of charitable funds, Evelyn found relaxation in studying French and practicing on her 1920 Steinway baby grand. Together they enjoyed social activities with a circle of friends and a growing collection of classic books. Shorty developed interest and skill in gardening, made possible by yard space that was extensive by city standards. When they retired to Florida, Shorty had a new climate and more space for his horticulture, Evelyn had more time for French and the piano, and together they had a pleasant social life at home and at beach clubs.

In my boyhood Shorty was chiefly an indirect influence. Mother was so displeased with the five years that Shorty took to graduate from high school and also with the five years that Grace needed, that I was warned to concentrate on my studies. On the way back from the war, Shorty thought up the idea of taking my girl friend away from me, but he was disappointed to learn that, at the age of 15, I had a number of excellent friends among the girls in my classes but no Girl Friend.

When I followed Shorty to Union College I was, from the point of view of Shorty's Psi U brothers, incredibly naive. I was blackballed, which Shorty took as a personal insult. From New York he wrote me a series of letters in much the same spirit as Lord Chesterfield's letters to his son, covering clothes, grooming and how to get along with associates of differing beliefs and life styles. I followed his advice, minded my own business and in a few months was able to accept a bid to join Psi Upsilon.

In the following years Shorty was very hospitable, whether I was staying with him in his bachelor pad on Fifth Avenue at 23rd Street (wonderfully quiet after business hours) or in the apartment he shared with his wife in Greenwich Village and later in an apartment in the Bronx. I remember wonderful lunches in which he introduced me to the delights of raw clams and oysters as well as a Sunday breakfast at Delmonico's with Evelyn as a charming participant.

MY SISTER GRACE

When the DuBois family moved to Catskill Grace was eleven going on twelve, and about to blossom into womanhood. And blossom she did; in fact Father's pet name for her was "Blossom." A sophisticated and much traveled middle-aged gentleman of Catskill was reported to have remarked, "She looks like the daughter of an English earl, by Jove!"

Grace had lots of girl friends at school, many of them visiting her at The Ridge. Dorothy Jones, Edward's older sister, was a frequent companion, along with "Tubby" Heath, "Connie" Wardle and "Tot" Van Orden.

Her greatest scholastic achievement in high school came in her senior year when she won the prize for excellence in Latin.

From time to time she gave parties at The Ridge. There was a Halloween affair with bobbing for apples, in which participants tried to retrieve an apple floating in a tub of water, using only their teeth. Much laughter, much splashing and much mopping up. By this time boys of her group were often coming to The Ridge.

Grace and Mother shared the use of an upright piano in the parlor. Grace practiced in accordance with her lessons with Mrs. Fox and became reasonably competent on pieces such as those making up Ethelbert Nevin's "Day in Venice."

Grace had a high school romance with a young man who lived on the other side of the river. The romance eventually came to an abrupt end, but while it was in progress she and the young man whom I shall call Jim were accustomed to leave notes for each other affixed to a large oak tree along the road leading to town.

While they were still engaged, Jim came to Grace very upset. It seems that his dates with a girl east of the river had involved intimate activities; she was pregnant; Jim and the other girl would have to get married. Grace was devastated, chiefly by the sudden loss of faith in Jim.

Had the telephone been known in the time of Romeo and Juliet, a long distance call would have solved the complications. Somewhat similarly and with modern medical skill available, Jim might have insisted on proof of pregnancy before marrying the girl. He didn't. The girl was not pregnant—her claim was just a ploy. Grace went on with her own life. However, her affair with Jim deserves a footnote. Many years later on a visit to The Ridge Grace happened to notice a weathered bit of paper on the As-You-Like-It oak tree. It was a note from Jim! His marriage had been unhappy and if Grace were ever free again...

After high school Grace taught in a private school for a couple of years and then, during the American involvement in World War I, studied interior decoration at Teachers College in New York City. I don't think she ever complained to Dad about four years of college only for the boys in the family, but it was a flagrant case of sex discrimination as she was as capable intellectually as any of her brothers. For a time she worked with a New York firm that sold Italian art objects on Madison Avenue and in resorts such as Bar Harbor. She had the happy idea of starting her own shop on Nantucket Island, eventually married John H. Bartlett, Jr.(generally called "June"), a graduate in agriculture at what is now the University of Massachusetts and manager of a beautiful Nantucket farm, the largest on the island. The last time the six members of the DuBois family were all together was at her wedding at The Ridge the day of the 1929 stock market crash. (No connection, of course, just a coincidence.)

She and her husband weathered many storms characteristic of their island home, including a financial crisis involving her father-in-law's farm, which June was managing. Their gifts to Nantucket include three sons, one of them proprietor of what had been his grandfather's farm. It no longer produces milk but it provides summer visitors to Nantucket bountiful supplies of fresh vegetables and flowers.My relations with Grace were always special. She and her friends had some familiarity with the cultural world: concerts, operas, books, languages, and some of that familiarity became mine. Everett Irwin, with whom Grace had a long time platonic relationship, merits special mention. He was a rarity in Catskill, an avowed aesthete with lots of exciting accounts of musical experiences in New York.

At 14 I received a wonderful Christmas present: a folding Brownie. When I attempted pictures of the surrounding out-of-doors, Grace helped me order inexpensive prints of nature painters demonstrating principles of composition: Corot, Hobbema, Constable, Turner. For my first visit to New York Grace procured tickets for Balief's Chauve Souris at the Century Roof Theatre. It was an unforgettable evening with entrancing musical mini-dramas and, during intermissions, wonderful vistas of Central Park.

I still like the Blue Points and Chesapeakes on the half shell to which Shorty introduced me, but as my English professor at college remarked, "Intellectual pleasures are the best." Grace was a good part of my introduction to intellectual pleasures.

MY YOUNGER BROTHER

Harry, officially named Henry R. DuBois, Jr., has always had a wonderfully smooth temperament and a sense of humor, as well as unusual talent for friendship. It was through his knowing John Bagley that the Bagleys and the DuBoises formed their long-standing coalition. The same thing happened with the Hopkins family. Somehow Harry became acquainted with Pell Hopkins, who was about the same age, and soon the Hopkins house became almost as familiar to both of us as our own.

Play with Harry was amicable, although I remember him running once to Mother complaining "Philip hit me with a baked apple!" Note: The apple was nature-baked, not oven-baked. Together Harry and I devised an admirable solution to the problem of dividing pieces of cake or almost anything: it doesn't matter who divides as long as the other person chooses. Together we developed great skill in dividing equally.

By the time Harry was old enough to play in the school playground, there were no restrictions imposed by the family and Harry made the most of the situation. Friendships proliferated and athletic skills grew, although he never attained Shorty's football fame.

Shorty played very infrequently with his two kid brothers, but one time he drove us as a team of horses—I was "Bill" and Harry was "Jake." And "Jake" became a nickname so persistent that only his parents (and perhaps his sister) continued to call him Harry. When he came to Union College as a freshman, I was a senior who introduced him as "Jake." I should have consulted him about this, since I had used the transition to college as a chance to drop my own nickname of "Skibo," which I didn't like very well. That also had come from Shorty, a modification of the command "Skip," used to send me on errands.

All through school Harry and I were separated by two full grades, but Boy Scout activities brought us together as did a 28-mile hike. We knew in advance the hike would be a long one, but we measured it out on a government survey map only after it was over. All around Catskill there is wonderful hiking country—picturesque streams, country roads and of course the mountains. That day, carrying our lunches and a camera, we took the Cauterskill road to Lawrenceville which then was merely a geographical area at the foot of North Mountain. The winding road up North Mountain had been used years earlier to take visitors by carriage up to the Catskill Mountain House. In 1920, which was probably the year of our adventure, it was largely abandoned. Some of the time we followed it, at other times we saved steps by cutting through the laurel underbrush to the road higher up. There was no habitation above us, so we had no reason to hesitate in drinking water directly from the occasional mountain stream. Once we achieved the rim, there was a trail south to the Mountain House where, of course, we rested and looked over the kind of view which is commonplace today from an airplane but then was restricted to mountains. Beyond fields, patches of woods, streams, and low-lying hills we saw the Hudson from far in the north to far in the south and beyond.

By 1920 the Otis Elevated Railway, a cable route up the face of South Mountain had been dismantled, but the trestle was still intact and the right of way made for an easy descent almost to Palenville. By this time we were getting tired, but we resisted temptation to ask for a ride from the very occasional automobile. We trudged back to Catskill village and north on the Athens Road—completely weary but satisfied that we had met the challenge of a hike to the base of the mountain, up to the 2,000 foot level, down the mountain and back home. It was not to meet a Boy Scout requirement—we had both met that requirement long before—a mere 14 miles in one day.

Harry and I joined forces in one Boy Scout event. Our scoutmaster announced a knot-tying competition. We looked up knots in a dictionary and in a quick whirl out-tied all competitors and continued with an array that went well beyond the hitch and the bowline on a bight.

Harry was such a success as a helper in Smiths' grocery that years later Mr. Smith proposed his name for full-time employment with the Catskill Savings and Loan. He accepted, moved his growing family to The Ridge and made his career as president of an organization that became the Greene County Savings Bank. His gift for friendship was tempered with good business sense—the organization prospered, and when in a later year I walked about the village with him he seemed to know almost everybody and universally was warmly greeted.

MOTHER

Mother, Hattie C. DuBois, was born in Catskill and grew up there. She had a favorite story about her childhood. Around the old farm house where she lived with Aunt Hattie and Uncle Harvey there were no katydids, despite numerous trees including some magnificent willows. On a visit to relatives a few miles north, she captured a number of katydids, brought them back to the farm and released them. A hundred years later there were still plenty of katydids in the area where the old farm house stood.

Aunt Hattie supervised what in the 1870's and 1880's was an excellent education: grade school in a one-room schoolhouse followed by a full course at what is now Catskill High School. She also had music lessons, becoming proficient in semi-classical pieces: Leybach, Mendelssohn, Lange. Early in the morning while living at The Ridge she would often play one of her pieces, or play and sing at the same time. "Hark, Hark, the Lark" was one of her favorites. Mother encouraged Grace with her piano lessons, but she never attained Mother's level of proficiency.

After high school Mother taught for two years in a one-room school at Green Lake, ten miles or so northwest of Catskill. She boarded near the school and walked home for weekends and apparently she was able to save some money. Anyway, she went to New York, studied at Cooper Union, actually sold a couple of wallpaper designs but gave up the possibility of an artistic career in order to marry Dad, whom she had met in Catskill.

Mother sometimes used her skill in drawing little sketches to amuse her children. At Easter time there would be a delicious lemon pie with a skillfully delineated white meringue rabbit on top. The eye of the rabbit was a bit of cooking chocolate. Her aesthetic interests included tasteful pictures hung on the walls, and later, with Grace, she bought wonderful antique furniture at country auctions where, as often as not, the table or chair or bureau had been covered by layers of paint.

MOTHER'S COOKING

Mother had ultra-modern ideas about cooking. Lots of fresh vegetables, lightly cooked. Her children liked her salads with very simple dressing. Practically no fried foods, potatoes usually being boiled, mashed or baked. Chicken was fricasseed or roasted. A leg of lamb started out roasted, then cold sliced and finally small bits in natural juice on toast. Heavy gravy was never served. Beef was frequently a wonderful pot roast, large enough for slicing. Her roast beef hash was always excellent. Nothing like supermarket hamburger ever entered the house. Often instructed to bring home "a pound from the round, ground," I would watch Mr. Friss, the butcher, as he cut off a slice or two from an enormous leg of beef and put the meat through the grinder. It was apt to be used for meat loaf.

We bought most of our groceries at the grocery owned and operated by the two Smith brothers: sugar, flour, salt, canned fruit, rice, potatoes when the supply of home-raised potatoes was used up, and cheese. Ah, cheese! We called it "store cheese," and it was New York State white cheddar. When a new round of cheese (about eighteen inches high and three or four feet in diameter) arrived in the store any customer could have a taste because there was considerable difference from round to round. But I never encountered any that was not delicious.

When an A&P store opened in town, we found that it sold Shredded Wheat, two boxes for a quarter (12 biscuits in a box). This was less than the price at Smiths', so whenever Shredded Wheat was needed, I would go to the A&P. The manager would sometimes call out "Shredded Wheat!" when I appeared in the store, but I always persisted in my defined, limited errand.

We did have lots of desserts. In addition to lemon meringue, pies were made from fresh apples or a fresh pumpkin, with mince pie at Christmas. There were no mixes available for either pies or cakes and I doubt whether Mother would have used them even if they had been carried in the grocery stores. She made a one-egg mocha cake (from a recipe which she found in a magazine and for which she used two or three eggs), an apple sauce cake which was a sort of ginger bread with lots of apple sauce, chocolate cake, sponge cake and, Dad's favorite, a coconut layer cake. The sponge cake was sometimes beautified with strawberries or whipped cream.

Bread was always home made, Mother never using a recipe. It disturbed the pharmacist in Dad to see her take an unmeasured amount of flour and bits of this and that, and put bread dough together. When he retired to The Ridge he took over the breadmaking, measuring all ingredients carefully. It was always good bread, but never better than Mother's.

We always had four quarts of milk a day, fresh from the cows on the farm. The only processing was cooling, no pasteurization! What we didn't drink or use on cereal was used in cooking: rice pudding, bread pudding, cheese souffle.

In the pantry there was always a box of salt codfish which appeared on the table as creamed codfish served with potatoes and a vegetable. Once in a great while there were soft-boiled eggs for breakfast but usually there was oatmeal or Cream of Wheat or a cold cereal such as Shredded Wheat. Available fruit for breakfast was seasonal, except for bananas. She would have liked frozen orange juice but the revolution caused by the introduction of frozen foods was yet to occur. Canned milk was available in the pantry for cooking and emergencies. The abundant eggs often appeared on the table as omelets.

Usually there was canned salmon (30 cents a can) in the pantry but the Fulton Fish Market on Bridge Street had enormous fresh fish on ice; always a cod and often a salmon, from which the owner of the market would cut steaks on demand. Our friends in town had iceboxes, for which the iceman would deliver ice, but no such service was available as far from town as The Ridge. Accordingly, we usually would eat the fish the day it was bought. Clams were special. A notice would appear in the local paper stating when there would be a clam boat at a dock in the village. The boat would be a sort of a sloop up from New York under its own sail. From the enormous pile of live clams on deck we would take home a generous quantity from which Mother would prepare delicious clam chowder, Manhattan-style with canned or fresh tomatoes.

Without refrigeration economical housekeeping involved problems which Mother always knew how to solve, chiefly by what must have been within-the-head scheduling. Some food was kept in the dark and fairly cool cellar: a barrel of apples, rooty vegetables in a bin of dirt, perhaps some eggs in what was called water glass, and various fruits and jellies in mason jars. For day to day leftovers there was the "safe," a cupboard with a fine mesh screen to keep out flies.

An inflexible rule of the house was that Mother was to have nothing to do with preparing Sunday night supper, which was sometimes a shared affair with Mother as "guest," and sometimes everybody finding suitable leftovers or a bowl of cereal. But Mother's self-assigned duties went far beyond preparing meals. Only when Grace was in the house did she have much help with dishwashing or cleaning. The boys were expected to keep their rooms picked up and their toys put away, but no one suggested that they could make their beds or sweep the floor.

They did help with the laundry (with pay set at 5 cents a batch). Mother had a clothes washer, a tub with two devices: a wheel which moved an internal mechanism back and forth, and a clothes wringer. A "batch" consisted of an agreed number of turns of the wheel followed by operation of the wringer. Pay might amount to 15 cents for half an hour of work. Except in the coldest weather, Mother hung the clothes on an outdoor line.

THE MONDAY CLUB

The Catskill Monday Club consisted of mature women who met regularly on Mondays to listen to papers presented by members. Membership was by invitation, with guests occasionally present at meetings. Mabel Root, Mother's life-long friend, was an enthusiastic member and asked Mother to attend as a guest from time to time. Again and again Mother declined Mabel's request that she be allowed to nominate Mother for membership. Mother had two reasons for her refusal: While the children were still at home she felt she did not have time to attend the meetings regularly, and she had fears about her ability to present an acceptable paper, especially since many of the members were college-trained.

Finally Miss Root won out. Mother's obligations at home had become less time consuming and she was persuaded that a paper, which would come only once in a while, would not be too formidable a task.

Presenters had an almost unlimited choice of topics, the chief restriction being that it had to be selected a long time in advance. In those years Ramsay MacDonald was at his peak in British politics, articles about him were abundant, there was considerable interest in his career, and Mother became an ardent admirer. She wrote and presented at least two papers on MacDonald to the Monday Club. They were so well received that fears evaporated and she became a confident participating member.

THE LATER YEARS

In the fall of 1924 Harry entered Union College and was the last chick out of the nest. Mother was alone at The Ridge for a few months until Dad could dispose of the Newburgh store and retire. In the years that next came along, they led a quiet but fulfilling life, with frequent visits from their children and their children's families, and more participation in community affairs than hitherto. During duck hunting season, Shorty and Evelyn drove up on Saturday nights from Westchester County. At The Ridge there was usually a cake waiting. Next morning Shorty would hunt ducks on the river with Milton Fredenburgh, while

Evelyn would rest and make herself pleasant company. In the middle 1930's Jake and his wife Betty would drive up from Peekskill, at first bringing David, and later David and Joan. In time Mother would say, "I love all my grandchildren equally, but David was the first!"

There were visits back and forth to Nantucket Island, where Grace and Junior were raising three sons. In my five years in New York, between teaching in Beirut and an appointment in Pocatello, I visited The Ridge from time to time and spent one summer there chopping wood and reading for my Ph.D. prelims.

Dad participated fully in domestic chores, read a great deal, resumed his interest in Masonic meetings and participated in church activities, serving on the consistory, first as a deacon, later as an elder.

EVENTS AND NON-EVENTS

THE RIDGE AND THE PINE LOT

After Dad gave up his attempt at farming, the farm was rented to Willis Brazee who, with his wife Minnie, eked out a modest living from it for many years. The Browns and DuBoises retained the new house and some five surrounding acres, all of which became known as The Ridge. By the time the house was built the surrounding maple trees seemed quite large. All but one resembled sugar maples, the exception being a magnificent Norway maple just outside the ring of trees close to the house.

From the kitchen there was a tiny view of the Hudson about four miles away. We could see the beacon in Brandow's Bay and beyond to a part of the river between Athens and Hudson. From the large plate glass window in the front room one could see a magnificent panorama of the entire range of the Catskill Mountains. Relative to the mountains, The Ridge is at a unique point: on the longest day of the year the sun sets just north of Windham High Peak, the apparent north end of the range; and on the shortest day of the year the sun sets just south of Overlook Mountain at the apparent south end of the range. In his retirement Dad loved to follow the procession of sunsets up and down the range.

Especially from outside with few intervening trees the view of the mountains is spectacular. On clear days many details could be noticed such as cable cars going up and down on the Otis Railway. In winter it often snows on the mountains before snow falls in Catskill. The blues and purples are stunning, and sometimes the cloud pattern is such that the detailed outline of Kaaterskill Clove, the cleft in the range leading to Haines Falls, becomes apparent.

Often the Catskills as seen from The Ridge are very, very blue.

When our daughter was very young, my wife and I had taken her to her grandfather's house for a visit. "Take me to the blue mountains," she demanded. We drove her out to the mountains where she was soon among green trees. To our astonishment she began to cry, saying amid tears, "But I wanted to go to the BLUE MOUNTAINS!"

About 600 yards away from The Ridge and over on the west side of Athens Road was the home of the man we called Judge Kerr, our nearest neighbor. He had been a justice of the peace and had served a term in the state legislature. Their spacious yellow and white frame house welcomed guests, "summer boarders," mostly from early June through Labor Day. The guests could play tennis or croquet, read and talk on the veranda, stroll through the woods, or walk to Catskill village for such excitement as a town of 5,000 inhabitants could offer. In all of Greene County, housing and feeding summer visitors was (and still is) a thriving business, and accommodations ranged from simple farm houses to elaborate hotels like the Catskill Mountain House, which was high on the range and easily visible from The Ridge. Kerr's visitors were mostly from New York and northern New Jersey, and many were repeaters. There was little for youngsters to do at Glen Mary, as the Kerr establishment was called, and apparently the suggestion was sometimes made that the two boys who lived on the hill across the road might be available as playmates. Neither Jake nor I took any initiative in the matter but a number of boys in our age range became friends after some screening by Mother. In an indirect way we became familiar with big city life but neither Jake nor I ever envied our new friends, least of all for living in New York or in urban New Jersey.

About 200 yards south of our house was the line, marked with bushes, trees and a wire fence, separating The Ridge from the next property, a pear orchard that was part of the Hopkins farm. In this part of Greene County apples and pears could be shipped by boat to a commission merchant in New York who would sell the fruit and remit the proceeds less commission to the farmer. Other crops such as fresh corn and berries were sold locally. I made my first wages, five days' work at $2 a day, picking pears in the orchard close to The Ridge. Only green pears were harvested, since only hard pears could be shipped.

FUN IN THE PINE LOT

A hundred feet or so north of the house was an old stone wall separating the house lot from the Pine Lot, somewhat over four acres in size and used as a cow pasture. It included three clumps of large pine trees. On the south side of the wall was a large patch of wild roses, single petaled, white and fragrant. Although they did not last long after they were picked, Mother loved to have a wild rose bouquet in the house.

There was a stile—later replaced by an opening too narrow for cows—in the wall by which we could go to the summit, with a small circle of trees apparently intended originally for a "summer house" or gazebo. Here was our favorite place for family picnics. The vista was magnificent, encompassing views both of the river and mountains. The Pine Lot was a favorite place for games, for sitting around a fire and for roasting potatoes. Underneath the trees was a thick carpet of pine needles.

We used dead branches from the pine trees for all our fires. Outdoors the pitch in the smoke is not objectionable and neither is the fact that the wood burns quickly. We roasted potatoes in a mass of embers, unmindful of the black outer shells—the interiors were delicious. (We never considered bringing butter and salt to the Pine Lot.) Our fireplaces were built of Normanskill shale, blue when first broken but grey when weathered. All our stones were weathered, picked up in the lot.

Jake and I christened certain features of the Pine Lot. King Spring was a small hollow under the brow of the hill. In very wet weather it accumulated some surface water—we soon discovered it wasn't a spring at all, but we kept the name. In the middle of the Pine Lot were some pines on an escarpment which became Harry's Woods, while Philip's Woods was at the north end of the area and included what we called the Cliff, a rocky place where some years before someone had dug out a quantity of rock, probably for road use.

The summit of the Pine Lot had a sharp escarpment on the east side with an old wild pear where the incline flattened out. Near the top of the pear tree hornets began a nest which grew and grew, providing a wonderful target for boys on the top of the hill only thirty feet away and who had available a goodly supply of small stones. The sport lasted for weeks as various friends joined the DuBois boys in trying to hit the hornets' nest with a rock. When we came near or hit the nest lightly, hornets would come out and buzz angrily but nothing else happened. Then came the day when our barrage of stones actually knocked the nest out of the pear tree. A swarm of hornets flew straight at us. We fled north but the hornets followed. I don't remember whether others were hurt but I was stung on the back of my neck. I succeeded in brushing the insect off before the stinger was fully implanted but even so the welt was half the size of an egg and very painful. At least one hornet had its revenge and I learned, as my father had told me, "Hornets pack a wallop!"

FISHING

There was no water for fishing on our premises. Occasionally Jake and I would dig a few worms and each would take his rod, hook and line to Town Line Creek a few hundred yards north of the farm house. This is a sizable stream in the spring, flowing gently in the summer. I never saw it completely dried up. Between the highway and the river are a number of pools, not large enough or deep enough for swimming but loved by chub and horned dace, the big ones being six or seven inches long. We would take a few home and clean them so that Mother could cook them for us. We never had enough for a real meal. The creek quite close to the river had a point of special interest, the remains of what we took to be an old mill where the stream had a drop of a few feet. If there had been a water wheel, it was no longer in evidence.

One time Becky Hallenbeck showed us how fishing in Town Line Creek should have been done. He had gone up and down the creek and was bringing home an unbelievable string of pickerel, some over a foot long. We didn't know that such big fellows existed there and he may have caught most of them. He found them hiding in the kind of pool we fished in, but by that time Becky was a grownup and an adept fisherman.

ONE O'CAT

We never had a diamond for any type of baseball. All that was necessary was a reasonably level space and improvised markers for bases. When there were eight or nine boys who wanted to play baseball, two captains, self-appointed or by consensus, would toss for first choice and then choose team members in turn. With four or five on each team there could be a battery of pitcher and catcher, two or three baseman, and with greater numbers, a shortstop and players in the outfield. The only regular rule we followed was three outs for an inning at bat. Since we had no umpire, there was never a called strike or a base on balls. The pitcher kept throwing until the batter made three unsuccessful swings at the ball (including fouls for the first two strikes) or a fair hit. If the ball went straight over the plate and the batter did not try to hit it, it just didn't count one way or the other. Sometimes it was agreed in advance to play five innings or so; usually we stopped when it was time to go home. Score was kept in everybody's head.

More likely, there wouldn't be enough boys to form two teams. No matter. With three or more it was always possible to play one o'cat, a wonderful game in which the batter plays against everybody else. There is only one base, off to the right of the batter. If a game is proposed, often with a designation of the proposer as batter, other players shout to get their positions. First call gets the slot. The sequence might be: "Let's play one o'cat, I'm batter." "I'm pitcher." "Catcher." "First base." "Shortstop." "Outfield."

The batter tries to make as many runs as possible before being caught out, or having three strikes before or after a run. Balls do not count. As in baseball, a foul ball is counted as a strike except that a third strike cannot be a foul. For a run the batter must hit the ball within what would be the limits of a diamond and run to the base and back.

When the batter is out, players rotate. The batter takes last position, outfielder if there is such. The pitcher becomes batter; the catcher becomes pitcher; the first baseman becomes catcher, and so on. One of the best features of the game is that a newcomer can join at any time—in the lowest ranking position. The game stops when it's time to go home or the players get tired.

CROQUET

The purchase of a croquet set was probably Grace's idea. It was set up under the maple trees on the lawn just south of the house, despite the fact that the ground was level only approximately. At least for the first season, Grace and her girl friends had lots of fun playing in the shade. Everybody followed rules that were probably standard for the game, one of its most appealing features being that any number can play up to the limitations of the equipment.

Shorty was soon demonstrating ruthless effectiveness, and Harry and I had no difficulty in learning the rudiments of play. The equipment was set up under the trees year after year, permitting many a pleasant friendly round. Finally the wooden balls became wobbly or broken and at that time there was not enough interest to warrant the purchase of a new set.

SLEEPING OUTDOORS

Summer weather can be very hot in Catskill despite boarding house claims to the contrary. Air conditioning was unknown and at The Ridge we had no electricity for fans. To avoid heat trapped indoors and to take advantage of breezes, the two young children might establish themselves on the balcony built over a part of the large front porch. To reach the porch we had to climb through a bedroom window, taking with us a mattress, pillows, sheets, perhaps a light blanket or two, and citronella, to be smeared on faces and arms to ward off mosquitos. Usually older individuals found the indoors preferable to the discomforts of the balcony.

A large tent had better acceptance and was used for years. It was owned by the WCTU for use at the country fair in Cairo, but Aunt Hattie was the custodian and somehow this private use was tolerated. Pitching the tent, which was quite large, involved a set routine of adjusting poles and canvas, raising the poles and holding them upright until stays could be attached to pegs. Uncle Harvey and Aunt Hattie never indulged in outdoor sleeping. I don't remember how other grownups slept, but Harry and I used army cots. The tent was reasonably cool, it was easy to open the sides, and much of the day it was in the shade of the Norway maple.

Later, after Grace had left home and Harry did not seem to be interested, I established a wonderful summer sleeping place on a large cot kept all summer long in an out of the way north corner of the front porch. As with the other outdoor sleeping places, I could see something of the stars and breathe the cool night air. And on rainy nights it was easy to retreat indoors.

WINTERS AT THE RIDGE

The house at The Ridge was somewhat sheltered from north winds by the summit of the Pine Lot and by the surrounding maple trees. Construction, however, was far from windproof: clapboard outside, plaster walls inside, single pane windows. On a cold windy night there were breezes coming in around the windows. The large bedroom occupied originally by the Browns had a hot water radiator bringing heat from the anthracite burning furnace and the bathroom had a register in the floor through which some warm air came up from the kitchen. Stairs, hallway and three bedrooms were unheated. We survived, thanks to lots of warm bedding, flannel night clothes, slippers, and flatirons heated on the stove, then wrapped in plenty of cloth and placed at the foot of the bed and inside the covers. Zero temperatures outside and freezing temperatures in the bedrooms were causes of remarks but not of complaints.

At night kerosene lamps were the principal source of light, with candles and flashlights decidedly secondary sources. For the dining room table and other places where people would gather there were large lamps with circular wicks that dipped into the glass reservoir holding the kerosene. These lamps were seldom moved while lit and then only for short distances. The small lamps with single wicks were considered portable and were standard in bedrooms. All lamps required care: filling the reservoir, trimming the wick and cleaning the glass chimney. When lit, the flame was adjusted by turning a simple mechanism which moved the wick up or down. Lamps were lit with matches and extinguished by lowering the flame and blowing it out.

When Jake took over the property in the 1940's, physical arrangements were modernized: electric wiring and adequate heating throughout, an unfailing supply of artesian well water, a fine bathroom upstairs and a downstairs powder room. The parlor and the dining room were combined into a large living room, and the front hallway which had been space largely unused designated as the dining room. The cellar was converted into a basement, and the fireplace which Mother had always desired was built in the living room. These new arrangements certainly made The Ridge more comfortable and they would have been welcomed earlier; but in the early part of the century our life was luxurious compared with that of the pioneers.

THE ATTIC

A door on the second floor opens on a wooden stair leading to the attic, which could have been finished into rooms had there been a need. Instead, it was used as storage, for such items as a marble foot bath which had been used for bathing all the DuBois babies and which looks much like an object in one of Mary Cassat's paintings. It is now an antique treasured by my wife. Another stored object was a huge walnut cabinet (called "armoire" in French) that Grandfather Anson, in accordance with French precedent, had probably used as a clothes closet. After it was shipped to Missouri in the 1940's, shelves were added and it now holds my photographic archives.

There were a couple of old trunks in the attic, one of which had been left in Aunt Hattie's care by a relative some twenty or twenty-five years before. It was deemed abandoned property (I think after contact) and opened. The most interesting object was a newspaper published in Kingston, N.Y., and reporting the death of George Washington. It seemed to be genuine, but later I learned that it was probably a reprint. The other trunk was Uncle Harvey's, which during his lifetime had been off limits to every one. After his death, Aunt Hattie opened it and discovered a picture which so shocked her that she immediately ran to the stove to burn it. After further inspection I was allowed to rummage through the contents and found various papers relating to business transactions that had interesting revenue stamps which Aunt Hattie gave me for my collection. She also permitted me to keep a couple of examples of United States fractional currency issued during the Civil War, one for ten cents, the other for twenty-five. During the war such notes had been known as "shin plasters."

A box filled with postcards received by various members of the

DuBois family was of more recent origin. Also in the attic were chairs and various items of clothing, including some of Aunt Hattie's that perhaps dated back to the time before she was married in the 1860's.

The attic was used as play space only occasionally, the most attractive area being a small loft that could be reached by climbing up on the wooden cases containing the unused milk bottles that Dad had ordered in connection with the milk route which he found necessary to abandon.

SURROUNDINGS OF THE RIDGE

Between the house and the Athens Road (connecting the village of Catskill with the village of Athens) there was a meadow with grass which grew tall enough to be cut for hay once each summer. Along the road was a hedge of bushes and a few trees including a pine and a large elm. To lighten up the landscape in the spring Mother planted dogwood and "shadblow," a tree growing twelve or fifteen feet tall with a profusion of tiny white blossoms that were supposed to herald the springtime arrival of shad in the river.

A winding road led from the highway up to the house, past a large planting of assorted flowering bushes, including lilacs, all this the work of Aunt Hattie. Leading south from the kitchen door was a rose arbor built by Grandmother's husband, Al Clough, of juniper trees cut in the Pine Lot. Aunt Hattie and Mother shared in the planting and care of the rose arbor, which in some seasons had abundant blooms of Dorothy Perkins roses.

DAD'S AUTO

Al Clough also built a windowless structure with large doors northeast of the house that for years was called "the garage" but eventually became a tool shed often called "the garden house." Its history involves Dad's attempt to find a good solution to his problem of long hours in a drugstore with no clerk to relieve him and the need to be with his family four miles away but over an unpaved country road. He decided to buy an automobile—the first in our vicinity. A Mr. Herr in Athens sold him a red Brush runabout completely open with a driver's seat for two people. All this was happening about 1911 before driver's licenses were required, and apparently the deal was closed before Dad had much instruction on automobile operations. The situation was complicated by the fact that Dad had little interest or skill in mechanical matters. As a pharmacist his training was in chemistry and physiology. However, probably with Mr. Herr assuring him that he would have no difficulty, he and Shorty, then about 17, took off in the car one Saturday evening for the trip from Athens to The Ridge. The road was not only dusty but had many curves and several steep hills. About half way down the road, the lights failed and from then on the trip took on aspects of terror. But the trip was completed and the little car even made it up the hill to the house.

Came Sunday afternoon—plenty of daylight so that the failed lights would not be a problem—and it was time to return to Athens. The Brush did not have a self-starter, it had to be started with a crank in front. The first attempt failed and so did numerous subsequent attempts. With increasing frustration, Dad finally walked over to Kerr's across the way, and made a telephone call to Mr. Herr, who eventually came down and succeeded in starting the car. Dad drove it back to Athens, put it in its allotted covered stall behind the drug store and for some years didn't touch it. I took a look at it from time to time when I rode to Athens on my bicycle. As families in our vicinity acquired cars and boasted about them I felt secure in knowing that the DuBois family already owned one. Finally Dad sold the car to someone with greater mechanical aptitude and thereafter it tooted around Athens without incident.

The empty "garage" became the place where Jake and I and our friends presented plays, charging 2, 3 or 4 pins for seats. Such was Aunt Hattie's passion for thrift that she always bought the cheapest seat.

FURNITURE AT THE RIDGE

When Dad and Mother were married in 1893, Dad's income was $18 a week and they acquired children faster than furniture, the children coming almost exactly two and a half years apart. The furniture they moved from Newburgh to Catskill was adequate, but I think Mother was proud only of the dining room buffet with doors opening on storage compartments. Later, however, Grace and Mother attended numerous country auctions and acquired some fine antiques at bargain prices.

Several nineteenth century blue and white coverlets also should be mentioned. The story was that itinerant weavers would stop at farmhouses to weave coverlets from accumulated wool. Some had woven inscriptions, such as "Manufacturing and agriculture are the foundations of our democracy." The leafy designs were folk art at its best.

PETS AT THE RIDGE

The three most memorable pets at The Ridge were Jacky the Cat, Jocko the Parrot and Pete the Airedale. We had had cats earlier but, when it came time for another, Mother had an offer for a yellow kitten from her friend, Mrs. Heath. Margaret, the oldest of the three Heath girls, was a friend of Grace, and Charlotte, the youngest, was in my class and a favorite partner for a waltz when we happened to attend the same dance. It fell to me to go over to the Heaths' and bring the kitten home. The trip must have been more than three miles each way: over the crossroad to King's Highway, south through Jefferson and on to the Heath estate near Catskill Creek. I traveled on my bicycle and on the way home I carried the kitten in a small round basket on the handle bar. It was a long trip with no difficulties. Jacky was soon part of the household. He was very friendly, grew to good size, and soon demonstrated his skill as a hunter. He cleared the house of the occasional mouse, and loved the abundant meadow moles outdoors. Rabbits were a specialty. After a kill he would eat as much as he could and come back to the house holding on to the half-eaten rabbit with his teeth. The rabbit would be carried between his front legs, resulting in a deliberate and somewhat awkward gait. The half-eaten rabbits disturbed Mother somewhat but not as much as the dead garter snakes he would bring once in a while. Jacky lived many years at The Ridge—at least fifteen—always very friendly to everyone and always very independent when he decided to go hunting.

JOCKO THE PARROT

Jocko the Parrot belonged to a family that vacationed at Kerr's across the way. The Mullers came from New York and a son about Jake's age was proud of a Cartagena parrot, which, when not spreading its wings, was all green except for a yellow patch the size and shape of a dandelion on the top of its head. We saw the parrot and its owner at Kerr's a number of times—and just before the Mullers were to leave for New York the family offered the bird to Jake, even though their son was not enthusiastic about giving it away. Mother didn't want a parrot in the house—but Jake teased and teased, assuring her he would take care of it. After she relented the Mullers decided they would take Jocko back to New York after all. A few hours after the Mullers left we received a message from Amos Post's garage — "Come and get your parrot!" It seems that shortly after the Mullers started, their car broke down and they decided to dispose of it, take the day boat back to New York and leave Jocko and his cage for Jake, who was delighted at the turn of events.

I was in no way envious of Jake and his parrot, which I usually ignored. However, since Jake was not always available, I occasionally had to feed Jocko, give him fresh water and clean his cage. Then it gradually became apparent that I could do what no other family member could do—carry him around on my finger without getting a nip. By reason of my being adopted by the bird, Jocko became mine.

Jocko loved bathing. In warm weather he had his baths outdoors, but in the winter he was sprayed with a watering can as he stood in a basin in the kitchen. Although we would try to get him dry with a towel, he always shook himself vigorously at the end of the bath, resulting in droplets like a fine rain all over the vicinity. He had few words; the most recognizable phrase he brought with him was, "Supper ready, Laura." A book on parrots which we bought stated that their sex is very difficult to determine unless an egg is laid, which never happened with Jocko so that we assumed that some previous owner had affixed the name Laura on the basis of erroneous sex identification. To the Mullers and to us, Jocko was male.

Jocko and Jacky developed an armed truce, brought about in the early stages of their acquaintanceship by a nip or two on Jacky's tail. In warm weather we would let Jocko fly up in one of the maple trees. He developed an unfriendly greeting to strangers coming up the driveway: a loud "Go back!" We didn't teach him this phrase—in fact we were never able to teach him any words. So he must have learned it from an earlier owner. Mother and I developed a technique of retrieving Jocko from a tree whenever he was reluctant to come down, which was on rare occasions. She would pretend to punish me and I would pretend to object, both of us making considerable noise. Jocko would always fly down, apparently to protect me. The act worked perfectly, even one day when Jocko flew far away and landed high up on a tree in the Pine Lot.

Jocko loved to parade, wings with variegated feathers stretched out. This was his invariable response when he was out of his cage and someone operated the carpet sweeper. While he liked to make sounds of various sorts, he was not an especially noisy bird. Any time he could be quieted by putting him in his cage and covering it lightly. His diet was sunflower seeds almost exclusively, which we raised some years but usually purchased.

After both Jake and I had left for college, Mother tolerated Jocko for another year but made her feelings clear that he was something of a burden. Accordingly before leaving on a three year overseas assignment I told her that Jocko should be given away. She found an elderly couple to adopt him and more than once the couple reported, "He's a beautiful bird!" He was!

OTHER PETS

Pete the Airedale I knew by reputation and on short visits to The Ridge. About the time I left for college, Harry's suggestion that The

Ridge needed a dog was followed and the result was Pete, truly beautiful and with soulful brown eyes. I shall omit the numerous stories about Pete because for me they were second hand. He had, however, little training and less discipline. Mother found his eyes and posture completely appealing even after he had been naughty. He barked and ran after one automobile too many and that was the end of Pete.

Of other pets little need be said. When we arrived at The Ridge, Rex was there, a very old dog brought from the farm. I was discouraged from trying to share his doghouse. Rex himself soon disappeared. Then there was a succession of assorted cats, climaxed by Jacky. And a neighbor presented us with a beautiful Scotch terrier pup but his introduction caused Jacky and Jocko so much alarm that a few hours sufficed for his rejection, politely and firmly.

Chipmunks were abundant around The Ridge as well as a fair number of squirrels, yet Jacky never caught either. When he brought home a partially eaten robin, as he did once or twice, he was punished, and apparently he learned the lesson. We saw blue birds in the spring and crows all year. The numerous hummingbirds inspired Mother to compose a poem:

> "Ev'ry morn the hummingbird
> Comes to my delphinium."

She thought it should have more lines but Elizabeth Barrett Browning might have called it a translation from the Japanese.

FLOWERS AT THE RIDGE

Both Aunt Hattie and Mother loved flowers but in different ways. Aunt Hattie loved plants individually—she was not nearly as concerned as Mother with their arrangement in a garden. Aunt Hattie's collection of dahlias inspired our tenant farmer to remark, "What's so good about dahlias? You can't eat 'em!" She was happy for the leisure that permitted her to grow flowers for their own sake.

In the front lawn, right outside the dining room window, there was a flower bed, first with cannas bordered with salvias, then after a few years peonies and finally roses. In front of the house there was a fringe tree and, in the early days, snow ball bushes. After Aunt Hattie died in 1923, the flower garden was exclusively Mother's; she liked to work in it early in the morning before other people were astir.

WILDFLOWERS

Wildflowers abounded. In late spring there were three or four acres of daisies in the meadow east of the house lot. My brother and I once took a cart piled high with daisies down to the village. It seems that there was a hall to be decorated and that both Mother and Mrs. Jones had promised to provide daisies. Mother paid us, and when we came by Mrs. Jones' house, she happened to come out, saw all the daisies, thought we had gathered them just for her and a second payment came out of the blue. We didn't want to tell her that they were not her daisies so we accepted the money without trying to explain what for us was a complicated situation. I forget what we told Mother.

Mother had a book on wildflowers which she frequently consulted. One day I brought home from the Pine Lot a flower which I correctly identified as "geranium immaculatum," based on knowledge gleaned from Mother's book. Mother was surprised and pleased and praised my newly acquired expertise, but I never repeated my triumph. Mother, however, always seemed to know the botanical names of the wildflowers she encountered

At The Ridge Dad usually referred to flowers as "foo-foo," which was Grace's term before she could pronounce the real word. And I contributed to picturesque speech when, as a very young person, I came into the house one evening and announced, "Mama, the stars are litted!"

BIRDS AND BEASTS AT THE RIDGE

Birds were always abundant, but in my time at The Ridge there was no skilled birdwatcher. Crows we had all year round and they could be heard and seen even when some distance away. Aunt Hattie hated them because they dug up seeds in her garden. The return of robins in the spring was always welcome and the advent of the first bluebird noted with pleasure. The maple trees provided the robins with suitable nesting spots and later on the lawn we could see the young robins with their speckled breasts. All through the summer and well into the fall robins could be observed pulling up worms. The Hudson Valley is a great flyway for ducks and geese, which could sometimes be seen flying in formation overhead. Shorty never cared much for hunting animals but he began to hunt ducks on the river before he left for college and continued to do so until he retired from his Westchester County job and settled in Florida.

Around The Ridge there were lots of chipmunks, the most visible species of wildlife. There were a number of red squirrels and a few grey squirrels. Occasionally, we could smell a skunk. When he was 15, Shorty trapped a skunk in the woods in the middle of the flats, a part of the farm west of the railroad tracks. He (or perhaps Dad) shot the animal but the odor was persistent. Shorty cured the skin and sold it, but he never tried trapping again. One day, over on the Hopkins property the dogs, with much barking, cornered a defenseless woodchuck, and finally killed it.

There were garter snakes, but nothing dangerous. One of my friends reported seeing a rattler in the mountains but I never saw one in the wild until many years later when I lived in the Rockies. There were common and uncommon insects, including garden pests. Aunt Hattie's remedy for lice on chickens was daubing on some kerosene, which was very effective. (She also used a squirt of kerosene whenever she had a sore throat.) For people the mosquitoes were only occasionally annoying, as attempts to control breeding places were successful.

Pleasant sound came from three sources: katydids in the evening; cicadas who often left their abandoned shells on trees and sang long and loud in the sunshine; and "peepers" living in the swampy valley just east of The Ridge. Their sharp mating calls enlivened spring evenings. I never saw one, but my nephew, as a youngster, was adept at catching them and told me they look like tiny frogs.

Then there is the story of the bear. In the summer of 1907, while the new house was being built, there was a forest fire in the mountains and a wandering bear came into the area. The workmen called Jimmy Hallenbeck, the Hopkins' farmer down the road; Jimmy appeared with his gun and shot the bear. The veracity of the story was attested by the big bear rug in Jimmy's house.

VISITORS AT THE RIDGE

Dad grew up with two brothers. The older was Louis, whom we called Uncle Louie, and next in age was Uncle Arthur, for whom Dad worked before we left for Catskill and from whom he bought the drug store in Newburgh. Both visited The Ridge from time to time, usually with their wives, and at least once Uncle Louie brought his two daughters, Anna and Emily. Uncle Louie was a wonderful relative, never appearing without presents for the youngsters, including not-to-be-forgotten baseball gloves.

One evening when Uncle Louie's family and our family were chatting on the veranda, I moved my chair next to Emily's, and she moved her chair away. I again moved my chair next to hers; and again she moved her chair away. I just wanted to be companionable to a good looking girl three years my senior but she would have none of it. I always remembered the rejection and, curiously enough, seventy-five years later Cousin Emily spontaneously mentioned the incident. Uncle Louie liked to send us magazines as well as wonderful pieces of colored leather from a business in which he was employed but which disappeared when various types of leather substitutes were developed.

One time Uncle Arthur and Aunt Mame drove up from Newburgh 55 miles away in their new Model T. Uncle Arthur wanted to know how fast it would go, but he never could have learned about maximum speed with Aunt Mame as a passenger. He took Harry and me out for a spin, found a long stretch of level road with no traffic and instructed us to watch the speedometer while he stepped on the gas. Faster and faster we went, until the car would do no more. We reported the speed. Thirty-five miles an hour! Of course it would have done more had the road been paved, but in those days there were few if any paved roads in Greene County.

I was too young to be surprised when a man appeared at The Ridge whom Dad introduced as our Uncle Tuthill but Grace said she had never been more astonished in her life. It turned out that he was a son of our grandfather, Anson DuBois, by his first wife and therefore Dad's half brother. Dad welcomed Uncle Tuthill although there was an undisclosed reason why his name had never been mentioned before his arrival. He gave me an excellent piece of advice. I told him I planned to build a ladder. "Do it now!" he said. I didn't because at that time I lacked both skill and materials, but his advice has sometimes kept me from undue procrastination.

Both of Uncle Arthur's sons, Anson and Frank, visited The Ridge but at different times. Anson trained for the ministry but eventually had a career in vocational guidance. After long years at sea, Frank retired with his wife to a place along the St. Lawrence River. When I was teaching at Washington University a student came to my office to report that he knew my Cousin Frank and was well acquainted with his inexhaustible collection of stories about the sea.

A big event each summer was the visit of Marion Blodgett, who had lived next door in Newburgh. Her arrival on the Hudson River Day Line steamer was something to anticipate and, while she was Grace's guest, she was a friend to the whole family.

GRANDMOTHER CLOUGH

Grandmother Clough was rather frail and seldom walked the three-quarters of a mile to The Ridge. Her home at 75 Thompson Street was not only a good place to leave bikes and to eat lunch on rainy days, but also a place for all of us to stop in on trips to town, that is, all except Shorty. He had been reprimanded by Grandmother's husband for running across the lawn and vowed never to visit the place again.

Juliet Clough was born in the early 1840's, married Franklin

Clough, my grandfather, during the Civil War, and had two daughters by him, Aunt Ella and my Mother. After Franklin died at the age of 32, she married another Clough, Albert, who was the father of a daughter, Millicent, who was our Aunt Milly.

Although I remember seeing them in Newburgh, they seemed well established in Catskill when we arrived in 1908. Theirs was a two-story frame house with a big veranda in front and on the west side. In back was a shop where Al Clough did carpentry and also a gate by which one could get into Catskill Village Cemetery. Actually on Thompson Street there was a house between Number 75 and the cemetery but the Clough lot was larger, cut behind the neighboring house and had room not only for a lawn but also a garden.

Upstairs was a flat which for a few years was occupied by Aunt Milly and her husband, Mr. Barringer. On the main level a front door lead to the parlor. From there one could go to the sitting room, then the dining room, and finally the kitchen with another door opening on the backyard. We always entered and left by the kitchen door—everybody did—although there was also a side entrance into the dining room.

I never called Al Clough grandfather; in fact I don't remember calling him anything, although our relations were cordial. Mother called him Al. He was a skilled carpenter and came to The Ridge for whatever carpentry was needed.

Grandmother and her husband often had disagreements, chiefly about his work habits. Whenever the weather was unpleasant he would stay home even if a job had been scheduled. At one time Grandmother became so exasperated that she contemplated having "wife of Franklin Clough" put on her gravestone. My father told her that would not do at all, and she dropped the idea. Al Clough subscribed to a trade magazine, *Iron Age*, which he read regularly. In the sitting room was a bookcase with what he described as glass imported from France. He was very proud of the glass, and warned us to be careful of it. It may have been imported but it looked no different than any other glass.

In college days I used to stop in to see Grandmother almost every time I was home. Nearly always she gave me a couple of molasses cookies, the kind that we had with our vegetable soup and Postum on rainy school days. Apparently I called on her shortly before I left for Lebanon, because when I returned to The Ridge after an absence of three years I found two very hard molasses cookies in the pocket of a jacket hanging in my closet.

Grandmother passed away when I was teaching in Pocatello. Dad wrote me after the event. He said that she was so overcome by the idea of becoming ninety that she went to bed for a week—and died. Al Clough lived on alone. Aunt Milly did not like the idea but could not change his decision. She came up from New York to see him from time to time and paid the taxes on the house, because by that time his earning power was pretty well gone. After he died, the house was sold, the veranda was taken off and the house remodeled into four small apartments.

Grandmother's legacy included pleasant temperaments to her three daughters. Grace preserved her recipe for molasses cookies, but I doubt whether hers have ever tasted as good as Grandmother's did to hungry school children on a rainy day.

There remains the story of Paddy, a small black cocker spaniel. I suppose there was a time when Grandmother was Paddy-less, but I don't remember it. Paddy barked and barked at strangers, but was otherwise friendly. Grandmother, of course, loved him, and as a country girl gave him proper care. Eventually he became old, grey and enfeebled. I was commissioned to see that he had a dignified and painless end. Accordingly, I:

Led him on a leash to The Ridge, three-quarters of a mile away.
Tied him to a stake.
Shot him with Shorty's 12 gauge shotgun. He was knocked over and was apparently dead.
Shot him again at close range just to be sure.
Dug a hole.
Buried him.
Cleaned the gun.

All for 50 cents. Grandmother wanted to know if he had suffered. I assured her he had not.

Grandmother Clough and Aunt Hattie were sisters of course. They saw each other from time to time and were friendly without being close. Aunt Hattie was involved in causes, specifically prohibition and women's suffrage; Grandmother was not. Aunt Hattie knew of many things that were happening in the world; Grandmother did not. Aunt Hattie had raised Mother and was entitled to be a mother-figure; Grandmother was the motherly one. While Grandmother had a few flowers in her yard she was by no means a flower-lover like her sister nor did she ever work for an objective as exemplified by Aunt Hattie's striving for a new house by saving tiny amounts of money from the sale of cottage cheese.

When daylight savings time was introduced to save energy during World War I, Grandmother christened it "Foolish Time," and kept her clocks on "God's Time." Accordingly we always had to make a mental adjustment when we stopped in while daylight time was in effect.

Grandmother regarded herself as "frail," complaining of fainting spells from time to time. The doctor could find nothing wrong and my diagnosis decades later is that her trouble was nothing more than anxiety-based overbreathing that usually can be easily controlled. Aunt Hattie worked out of doors with vigor and enthusiasm, using a shovel or a pick axe when necessary. Grandmother outlasted Aunt Hattie by a dozen years and when she died at 90 Dad said, "A creaking gate hangs long."

AUNT MILLY'S WEDDING

Aunt Milly, daughter of Grandmother and Al Clough, and Theodore Barringer were married at 75 Thompson Street on July 11, 1911. It was a hot day!

Aunt Milly had been employed in a New York City school where Mr. Barringer, a widower, was principal. She was reluctant to marry a man approximately twice her age of 33; but she gave in and they were in Catskill for the ceremony.

Dad came down from Athens, walking the four miles. Aunt Milly sent a horse drawn cab to The Ridge and we rode to town in style. It was my first (and last) ride in such a vehicle. Several of us were crowded in the interior. The scenery was perfectly familiar since I had been going back and forth to school over the same route for a full school year, occasionally with a ride for part of the way. But this was an enclosed cab for special people on a special occasion. Needless to say, I was thrilled.

A year or two before I had been confused about weddings, which I had never attended, and the wetting at baptisms, which I had seen. By this time I knew the difference. Ten or fifteen guests, together with the minister and Mr. Barringer, were assembled in the rearranged dining room. There was music, and Aunt Milly emerged from a side room in her white dress. The ceremony proceeded, then came the reception on the same spot, with something to eat and some punch which the minister jocularly called "red ink."

Mr. Barringer was jovial and proposed a conundrum: "What city is 3/7 of a chicken, 2/3 of a cat and 1/2 of a goat?" As a successful first grader, I had read the conundrum a few days earlier and shouted out "Chicago!" Mr. Barringer was not amused.

The minister was a family friend, the Rev. Irving H. Berg of the Dutch Reformed Church, to which we walked almost every Sunday for Sunday school classes and church services. Later Mr. Berg resigned his Catskill pastorate to accept a similar position in one of the large collegiate churches in New York City which are part of the same denomination. Some 28 years later I was to encounter him again. He was then the dean of the undergraduate college of New York University at University Heights in the Bronx and I was there as a visiting assistant professor of psychology. He told me that when he was a pastor in Catskill he was really more prosperous than at any other time. His salary was $3,000, a princely amount in 1911. There was no income tax and the parsonage was rent free.

After his retirement Mr. Barringer continued to take great interest in public affairs and many of his letters "to the editor," typed by Aunt Milly, were published.

THE LITTLE GIRL WHO WASN'T THERE

At the age of four going on five I was on a sidewalk near our home in Newburgh when a white hearse, drawn by horses, went by. An older boy said to me, "Look, that's what they used to take your sister away." It was my first intimation of Marjorie. Later, in the front room at The Ridge, there was always a framed photograph of a smiling, curly-headed two-year old girl.

Mother rarely spoke of the little girl she had lost just a few days before she delivered me. Aunt Milly once remarked that at the time Mother nearly died of anguish. It seems that Marjorie had been gravely ill twice, once with diphtheria and finally with dysentery. (Had sulfa been known in 1903 a few tablets might have saved her.) Once Mother said to me, "I was very sad when you were born." And another time, "I had two curly-headed children, you and Marjorie."

A few years ago Grace told me that after Marjorie died, Sunday afternoons in suitable weather involved a family walk to Woodlawn Cemetery, with a baby in a perambulator. For a couple of years I was that baby.

I now speculate on Marjorie's indirect but perhaps very real influence. When I was six or so I asked my Father when we were going to have another baby. His reply was short: "There won't be anymore." Perhaps that indicates that if Marjorie had lived I would have been the final child; certainly her passing greatly changed the family constellation.

Another speculation. My health has been amazingly good through the years—in 20 years of active and reserve military duty, I passed all my physical examinations with no trouble— but a congenital malformation of chest bones was often noted. Much later, an eminent neurologist declared that a peculiarity in the bones of my feet was associated with a congenital deficiency in the functioning of certain peripheral nerves. It is possible Mother's stress in connection with Marjorie's diphtheria influenced my prenatal development. What is more certain is that, compared to my brothers, I have always been somewhat disadvantaged physically. I was never able to compete in a sport effectively even though I could swim, skate and play one-o'-cat with the other boys. In fact, one of my classmates at college once told me that a circus should hire me to imitate the clowns—my awkward attempts would bring bigger laughs than their regular antics.

I do think that very early I discovered a way to compete with my brothers by using a brain that was not necessarily any better than theirs but which was nonetheless quite effective. And the need to use it competitively may have been an indirect legacy from Marjorie.

NEIGHBORS UP AND DOWN THE ROAD

THE HOPKINS FAMILY

NEXT door to The Ridge was the Hopkins house. Actually it was several hundred yards down the road toward the village. Mary Pell Hopkins, who had a New York society background, was once a summer visitor at the Summit Hill House, where she met Samuel C. Hopkins, the son of a local doctor of some means. After they were married they settled into a somewhat pastoral existence in Catskill. In the front hall of their residence a copy of the New York Social Register listing their family was always next to the silver dish for calling cards. Someone wrote a novel about their romance but I know neither the title nor the name of the author.

There were two Samuels in the family, Sam Sr., and his older son, Sam. His sons like to say that Sam Sr. was the best first baseman Yale ever had. As far as anyone knows, the only work Sam Sr. had done in his life was on a ranch somewhere out West from which he'd brought home a pair of high-heeled cowboy boots his sons loved to wear when they were on horseback.

One story told by his sons: after dinner somewhere in the West he wanted to give the waiter a tip, pulling a coin from his pocket. He thought it was a silver dollar (a pretty good tip in the 1890's) but after the waiter thanked him profusely and walked away, Sam Sr. discovered he had given the waiter a $20 gold piece.

The Hopkins land was extensive. Most of it was woods and pasture, but some was planted, and next to The Ridge was a productive pear orchard, usually with buckwheat underneath the trees. The farmer was "Jimmie" Hallenbeck, who lived with his wife and son "Becky" in the tenant farmer's house up above the main residence and next to a large carriage house. On beyond was the "big pond," fed with rain water. It was a favorite place for the whole village to skate, a place for the Hopkins boys to row, and a source of somewhat odiferous water for the Hopkins bathrooms. Still further, on a high ridge which in some places overlooked the Hudson, were the very shallow "little ponds," which sometimes provided safe and satisfactory skating.

Becky Hallenbeck was about Sam's age but they did not usually play together. After Shorty received his commission in World War I, I remember him telling Becky how to get a commission after he joined the Army. The Hallenbecks made butter and it was often my assignment to walkover to their house for buttermilk, which they gave away. Theirs was the first larch tree I had ever seen.

Our intimate contacts with the Hopkins family began when Harry was perceived as a good playmate for Pell, the younger son. Since by that time Harry and I were playmates, I too became involved. Pell attended the Misses Cobbs' private school in their house on Thompson Street, which had existed for some time. A private school was consonant with the Hopkins life style—in the early part of the century private grade schools for those who could afford them kept their children isolated from the less opulent and perhaps, just perhaps, provided more effective instruction. After going through the grades with the Misses Cobbs, Sam and later Pell attended St.Paul's Preparatory School in Concord, New Hampshire, before entering Yale. The Misses Cobbs' school was so small that it did not provide Pell with a playmate. It did provide instruction in French, some of which Pell relayed to us: "oiseau" for "bird;" "taisez-vous" for "keep still;" and "tais-toi" for "shut up."

Until he was ten or so, Pell had a "nurse," Laura Cargel, who was much in evidence and probably was instructed to see that minute by minute events went well. She approved of Pell's owning a few shares of corporate stock. "All children should have some," she said. We had no idea of how to attain this objective. There had been some sort of a handyman on the place, but his only vestige was "Sawyer's Room," later torn down for an improvement I will mention later. The household included a maid and perhaps a cook; Mrs. Hopkins seemed to be free of routine household duties. She did not let her numerous social activities interfere with her interest in her children and what they were doing. At the appropriate time each week, Mr. Hopkins changed a round sheet of paper in the recording barometer on the front porch. This was his only observable function. He was an affable individual whose leisure was complete.

Mary Pell Hopkins loved to take photographs with her large folding Kodak. Several times Sam, Pell, Harry and I dressed up a bit to act out the sequence of a story which she developed. Once when I was supposed to be a Western bartender I was somewhat embarrassed when she had me wear one of her beautiful linen aprons.

We children went to tennis parties, which always included lots of nicely served refreshments. The generation a few years older played on the turf court on the huge expanse of lawn just south of the house. The grownups sat around and talked. We learned tennis rules and scoring and practiced a bit when the court was free.

It was a big event when the Hopkinses bought their first automobile, a Franklin touring car with a sloping front. We kids did not approve of the streamlining—a word we did not know—because we thought it cut down on the space for the engine. Jimmie Hallenbeck, the resident farmer, was unhappy because he was to drive the car in a chauffeur's uniform. But soon there were memorable excursions!

One summer there was an epidemic of infantile paralysis, as polio was known at that time. There were a number of cases in Athens, four miles to the north. One of the victims was Marian Herr, daughter of the dealer who had sold Dad his automobile and a friend of Grace's. In a time of fear, Mother and Mrs. Hopkins came to an understanding — the DuBois children would play only with Hopkins children and vice versa. None of us came down with infantile paralysis and we all got along just as usual, that is to say very well.

There were often interesting visitors at the Hopkins house. A neighbor was Clarence Howland, father of Billy and Louise who were schoolmates of Sam and Pell. Then there was Sam Sr.'s brother, "Uncle Charlie," a bachelor, somewhat precious in manner, but always with something to say that merited attention. Then there was Steven Pell, Mrs. Hopkins' brother, who had just bought Fort Ticonderoga. Her remark: "I don't know why Steve would want to do that." And Pell's comment after a visit to the fort was similarly unenthusiastic: "Not much there; just a couple of old cannon." A very attractive young visitor was Cousin Isabel Pell, whom I read about in *Time* when she emerged as a member of the French resistance as World War II was winding down. One of the Hopkinses' New York friends, a member of the Harkness family I think, decided that the Hopkins boys needed a billiard table. The family was glad to accept, but nowhere in the house was there a room large enough. The decision was made to build a new room. Sawyer's room was torn down to make way for a two-story addition, the second story being the magnificent billiard room: a beautiful hardwood floor, large windows with a mountain view, a fireplace surmounted with a fine portrait of Mary Pell. It was such a beautiful room that the idea of filling it with a billiard table seemed absurd and the original purpose was abandoned—instead it became a showcase family room. Many years later when Sam started to tear down the house as old and worthless, a young family persuaded him to keep the "billiard room" intact as the focal point of a new house they would build on the site.

In the early part of the century, boys generally wore short trousers or knickers until they were in one of the later grades. My height made short trousers somewhat incongruous and more than once I was asked by one of the older boys, "When are you going to drop 'em?" Opportunity came through the Hopkinses who gave me several pairs of long trousers which they had received as hand-me-downs from New York friends. And so it happened that my first long trousers bore a Fifth Avenue label.

Mrs. Hopkins was attractive in appearance and personality. She treated the two boys from up the road as semi-family members. We were sometimes invited to stay for lunch, where the food tasted no better than at home but was served in more lavish surroundings and with help from a servant. She provided Pell with lots of books and records, including Sousa marches as soon as they appeared and which Pell loved to play on his phonograph in the nursery. His possessions included all the volumes of the Book of Knowledge, which was an almost unlimited source of information, some of the classics and dozens of the Appleton writings, including the Rover Boys' books as soon as they were published. Her policy on lending books was generous—we took them home regularly and read them. The Rover Boys' adventures were generally implausible, but the stories were clean in thought, clearly written and stimulating, even though they gave me notions that Africa was mostly rain forest, that the Sargasso Sea was filled with deserted ships in danger of sinking, and that the Everglades were mostly saw grass.

The Hopkins house had a quiet air of luxury. Mrs. Hopkins supervised every detail: everything was clean and in good order with no hint of confusion. She obviously wanted her sons to have the best possible education: private school in Catskill, then St. Paul's and Yale. However, I do not recall discussion of vocational plans by any member of the family.

A big event came in 1913 when the entire family sailed to Naples on the Cunard Line. A card came back signed with a dagger and Sam's favorite nickname, "Half Breed." It was a special happening to see a card from a friend mailed with an Italian stamp. The sightseeing seems to have ended in England. On his return Pell, who was six or seven at the time, reported seeing Queen Mary. Apparently he had expected her to be wearing a crown but what she had on was "just an old hat."

As Pell grew into his teens, he entered into our circle of friends, participating in activities such as group hikes. I have a picture of Pell with some of my friends. It was taken on the third bridge of the Catskill Mountain Railroad, which means we probably hiked through Austin's Glen to a spot not far from Leeds.

For many years Sam had had older companions, but as they drifted away to college or to jobs, he began to share his enthusiasm for guns, horses and building projects with Pell, Harry and me. There was target practice with a .22 rifle for all. In a cowboy game with Sam on a horse, I was roped, Sam fell off, the horse ran away and I was dragged by the leg for fifty feet or so until fortunately the rope broke.

Sam conceived the idea of building a cabin in the area between the Hallenbeck house and the barn, just off the road leading to the big pond. Sam was the boss. He had excellent knowledge of how to put a building together, a supported floor, walls, windows, a door and roof. The result was almost a one-room house. I don't remember spending much time inside: the project was building the building and it demonstrated Sam's talents.

For years the Hopkins family life was idyllic but it ended tragically. One tragedy involved Pell. After St. Paul's he entered Yale, but after a time he was advised to take some time off and work for a while. While employed as a truck driver in Albany, be became ill with pneumonia and died. It was a great loss. His father became incapacitated with a stroke, and for months Mary Pell Hopkins devoted herself exclusively to his care. Then Sam Sr. passed away and, with an overdose of aspirin, it was likewise with Mary Pell. After St.Paul's, Sam of course had entered Yale where his greatest achievement was the captaincy of the polo team. Possibly he had connections that might have given him entry to a New York business career, but he became a floor salesman for a Spaulding store where he could capitalize on his knowledge of sports. Eventually he returned to Catskill and took over the family property. He got some cash income by working as a butcher (quite possibly a unique happening for anyone listed in the New York Social Register). More remuneratively, he sold parts of his property as building lots. The last time I saw him he had fixed up a part of the carriage house for bachelor living quarters. He died a few years later. Sam had a wife, who worked at a hospital in Poughkeepsie forty miles away, and a daughter, but they were not closely identified with Catskill. I do not know what has happened to them other than Sam's widow disposed of the remaining real estate after Sam passed away. It was at that point that the story of the Hopkins family that I knew ended.

What happened? The high-priced education which the Hopkins parents planned for their children would have prepared them for a pleasant life of leisure such as the parents enjoyed for many years. The family fortune dwindled so that at the time Sam was sole heir there apparently was little left except a large number of acres of not particularly productive farm land. Sam complained that Yale had not prepared him to earn a living—the tragedy was not Yale's failure but the supposition of his parents that he wouldn't have to.

THE THOMAS COLE ESTATE

On our way to the village of Catskill, the first house was the Hopkins'. Then came Howlands Lane leading to the home of the Misses Howlands invisible at the top of the hill. Then came the lot with the reservoir holding the village water supply, at that time pumped from the Hudson, and then the Cole Place: a large barn on the west side of the road, and on the east side the large white house of the famous painter, Thomas Cole, his studio and a smaller house. The land was extensive and included a large apple orchard extending almost as far as The Ridge. In earlier times apples had been shipped to England; in the 1920's they were harvested for the New York market.

Thomas Cole was, of course, long since dead. His son, Theodore, was a kindly old man when I was in the lower grades, often driving to and from the village in a buggy or, in winter, a sleigh with a foot warming device. When he overtook me on my way to or from school I was generally offered a ride. Our talk was always chit-chat.

Theodore Cole had two daughters in Catskill, Florence Vincent and Mary Emily Van Loan. I knew both but in very different ways.

Mrs. Vincent and her husband, Dr. Vincent, lived in the small house on the Cole Place. Later she occupied the large house with fine old fashioned furniture and a number of Thomas Cole paintings, which in those years were not in vogue. Somewhere John Ruskin had written: "Cole was a good painter for his time but his time was very bad." Many modern critics find his landscapes very remarkable; I particularly like his paintings of scenes I know. And of course I saw some of his paintings in the house in which he had lived.

One time I had an accident involving my nose. I was playing with Edward Jones in front of the Jones House. Edward jumped on my back, I fell forward and my nose hit the edge of the porch, a couple of feet above the ground. My nose was squashed. I was taken to Dr. Vincent's office. He squeezed and manipulated and pretty soon my nose was back in shape.

Some weeks later Dr. Vincent happened to make a house call at The Ridge. Mistaking one brother for the other, he got hold of Harry and carefully felt his nose. "I did a pretty good job on the nose, didn't I?" he asked. This was a great joke on Dr. Vincent.

Mrs. Vincent and Aunt Hattie shared enthusiasm for flowers, sometimes exchanging slips and bulbs, but at the county fair they became friendly rivals, vying for ribbons and related cash prizes. Both grew some flowers just to exhibit at the fair.

After Dr. Vincent died, his widow took over her father's house. She gave Aunt Hattie some of Dr. Vincent's medicine—she said she could not take money for it but she could give it away. It was the medicine Dr. Vincent had used with Aunt Hattie in the days when physicians regularly stocked medicines for their patients.

Mrs. Vincent established an antiques business with beautiful pieces of furniture she bought at auctions all over the area. Here Grace and Mother were sometimes her rivals—both knew quite a bit about antiques and bought tables, chests of drawers and chairs they could use. In later years Betty (Harry's wife) discouraged us from buying any of Mrs. Vincent's antiques, saying they were too expensive. Of course they were when compared to auction prices, but not compared to the going prices of other dealers.

Mrs. Vincent was happy when some of her land was sold for the western approach to the Rip Van Winkle Bridge. When she died there was disappointment in the Van Loan family, no member of which received anything. Instead the chief heir was Mrs. Howard Silberstein, the daughter of Theodore Cole's only son and the niece of both Mrs. Vincent and Mrs. Van Loan. There was a plan to turn the Thomas Cole home into a state museum. Mrs. Silberstein was willing to cooperate and made the house and the very valuable paintings available to the state at a reasonable price. There were too many delays and the paintings were scattered. After some years the museum was established but with a much smaller collection of art than it might have had.

I knew Mrs. Vincent's sister, Mrs. Van Loan, only through her dancing class, which I attended for two winters. In fact I did not know that the two women were related until years later. Ted Van Loan, her son, is my authority for stating that the fee was 25 cents a session and that there were different classes grouped by age. Usually there were 20 to 25 boys and girls at a session. In advance, Grace had taught me a little about dancing, showing me waltz steps while we sang Victor Herbert's "Come, come, beautiful lady." When the Van Loan class was announced, it was decided that I should attend. I did not need to be persuaded.

Individually we went to the Van Loan home on Prospect Avenue one night a week. Mostly we knew each other from school, but this was a wonderful chance to improve acquaintanceships. When a girl lived nearby no one called for her but a boy would walk her home. Mrs. Van Loan was a good teacher, often assisted by her husband—as suave a grownup as Catskill afforded. To the latest phonograph recordings, we were taught the waltz, the fox trot and the two step. There was also instruction in "jazz steps," in which the couple stood in place and moved feet back and forth in turn. The maneuver was probably ancestral to the Charleston. At the time the innovation was not particularly successful and I never saw any veterans of the class demonstrating "jazz steps" in a ballroom. However, we had fun, we became better dancers, and we developed friendships that made subsequent encounters at dances much more enjoyable.

NORTH OF THE RIDGE

Opposite the old farm house was a one acre tract with a dwelling which we called the Fenton House, occupied by the four Fenton sisters, one of them married to Mr. Truesdale, a piano tuner, and another a widow with a son, Bobby Tompkins, whom we knew well and with whom we occasionally played. On the same tract of land, years before, there had been a small house in which Grandmother Clough had lived with her husband, Al Clough, and her young daughter, Millicent. I have seen a photograph of my Mother as an adolescent, seated on the grass in front of the house, with the baby who became Aunt Milly in her lap.

WILLIS AND MINNIE

The DuBois family had a long and generally highly satisfactory relationship with Willis Brazee and his wife Minnie who occupied the old farmhouse year after year. Childless, they always had a large dog and several cats. It all started in 1909 when Dad discovered that the Brown farm would not support two adults and four children. Consequently it was decided that all the property was to be rented except The Ridge, which included what amounted to a hay field as a front yard west of the house, and the chicken yard and three or four acres of garden space toward the east.

Willis Brazee turned up as the renter. As during earlier days, the farm now had only two people to support. Rent was to be $20 a month for the farm house, barn and milkhouse, and about 50 acres of land, of which possibly half was arable. There were several patches of unproductive woodland. The Pine Lot where eventually Harry and I were to play was pasture, and there was more pasture west of the highway, capable of supporting a herd of 8 or 10 cows. Some of the arable land could be used for field corn and there was abundant land for hay. No one had planted fruit trees for decades so the pear trees and cherry trees were about to cease bearing.

The agreement with Willis involved his supplying the DuBois family with four quarts of milk a day at 5 cents a quart, the prevailing price in 1909. The DuBois children grew up on delicious-tasting unpasteurized milk, produced under conditions that could not possibly have passed any kind of inspection. The barn which Harvey Brown used for over 40 years and which Willis used for 25 years more was on the south side of the road still called Brown's Crossing. Across the road was a well, an old orchard and a hill with a magnificent mountain view. Down by the main road was the milk house with a well used for storing milk in 40-gallon cans. The farm house, kitchen garden and another well were on the east side of Athens Road, the main highway.

As one approached the barn from Athens Road there was first of all a section where wagons were kept. Then a door led to horse stalls on the left and more equipment on the right. In the rear there were stalls for cows, along with windows opening on the barn yard. Overhead was a loft from which both horses and cows could be fed. Finally at the west end of the building was an enormous hay mow. Outside there was a circular corn crib, with large tin collars on the supports to protect it against rats. Everything about the barn was functional from the wooden pegs for harness to the easily cleaned runways behind the stalls. There was, however, no running water. It had to be carried in buckets from a well across the road.

Many a time Harry and I watched as Willis and Minnie milked cows in the barn. Both were hard workers. Minnie exuded cheerfulness, addressing farm and domestic duties with equal zest. While Willis was by no means a sour person, his manner was always one of sparsely-worded determination. Neither knew very much beyond their narrow world of practical farming. When the First World War was at its height, Willis asked, "Who are these Allies, anyway?" pronouncing the key word like the plural of alley. "They seem to be the biggest country in the bunch." He was a member of the Order of Odd Fellows, and Dad helped him become a Mason, but had difficulty in teaching him the ritual. But join he did, and occasionally we would see him walking down the road early in the evening, dressed for one of his meetings.

Willis generally left our gallon milk can early in the morning on a peg on a telephone pole at the junction of the main highway and the road leading up to The Ridge. Sometimes milk was needed the night before so Harry or I would walk down to the farmhouse to get it. Sometimes we would watch Willis and Minnie operate their big cooling device. Willis would pour buckets of milk into a container with a top from which tiny streams of milk would flow down a truncated cone of gleaming stainless steel. Inside were chunks of melting ice. Minnie would pull again and again on a handle on a rod so that ice water would splash against the interior of the cone. The chilled milked flowed into a large can which was eventually lowered in the well where it stayed cool until transported to town.

When working nearby, Willis was quick to respond to any emergency we youngsters had when playing in the Pine Lot. Once George Bagley was hit in the head by a stone which bounced off a tree after someone threw it. (Maybe I did.) Anyway, George was bleeding and I ran over to the Brazee house saying that one of the boys had had his head bashed in. Of course it was only a superficial cut, but aid came, the bleeding was stopped and George went home for definitive treatment. Willis also came to our rescue with a rake when we accidentally set fire to the carpet of pine needles in one of the clumps of trees. Both times he made remarks about our need to be more careful in the Pine Lot.

At The Ridge we had regular contact with Willis when he stopped in to pay his rent—$20 a month less 20 cents a day for milk. As the price of milk advanced he complained more and more about the price of 5 cents a quart until Mother told him she would be glad to pay more but the rent would go up to $25 a month to cover the increase. He never raised the issue again. From time to time there were minor discussions about the property, but under the informal agreement it was his responsibility to keep everything in usable shape.

I was not in Catskill when, many years later, Minnie died. Dad said that after that event Willis was like a ship without a rudder—he just didn't know what to do. He finally decided to quit the farm and take a job as the farmer at a county institution. He held an auction. Dad retrieved one object that had belonged to Uncle Harvey—a beautiful grain scoop, a large shovel which had been hand-carved from a single piece of wood and was in excellent condition despite decades of use.

The new tenant was the gas maker at the local gas plant, so that farming was only part-time. He had two helpers, his wife and a somewhat mysterious woman who lived with them. Finally Mother decided to sell the farm, reserving only The Ridge, its surrounding acreage and the Pine Lot. The Pine Lot is now listed on the tax rolls as woodland, unimproved, while Jake inhabits The Ridge, along with his son and his son's family, which includes two children who constitute the third set of youngsters growing up there. As far as their Huguenot ancestry is concerned, they are of the eleventh generation in America and the ninth in Catskill. The boy carries the name of Joel, his great, great, great, great grandfather, a soldier in the American revolution who married his first cousin, Annatje DuBois, daughter of Col. Cornelius DuBois, under whom he had served.

Daisy Pickers: Harry and Philip.

A geology walk ended up at the Third Bridge: Pell Hopkins and Miss Root, with a trick pose by Edward Jones.

High above Kaaterskill Clove with Mary Vedder, Miss Root and Ruth Majilton.

Catskill, NY. Collection of Michael Walsh, The Village Pub, Catskill.

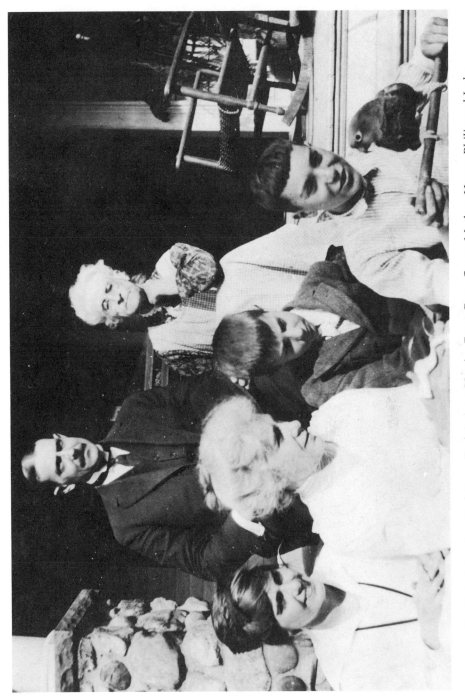

The DuBois family. Back Row: Dad & Aunt Hattie. Front Row: Grace, Mother, Harry, Philip and Jocko.

Aunt Hattie in her rose arbor.

Mother in her vegetable garden.

Grace amidst the iris.

Skiers trudging up the Pine Lot.

A snow fort at The Ridge. Robert Tompkins, Harry DuBois and Chancey Smith.

Weary Boy Scout hikers take a rest. Assistant Scout Master Ward McLaughlin is second from left, back row.

Harry and Philip.

RIVER, PONDS AND CREEK

THE HUDSON RIVER

I HAVE already noted that both from our house and from the Pine Lot one could see a patch of the river three or four miles away. To get to one of the ice houses or to one of the bathing beaches entailed a walk of a mile. It would have been much closer—a half mile or so—if it had been possible to travel on a straight line east, but various obstacles made such a route impractical.

From the time of early settlers, the Hudson was the great north-south route for sailing vessels and, after the time of Robert Fulton, for steamers carrying passengers and fast freight and for tugs pulling barges filled with goods of many kinds. In the early part of the century there were tiny local steamers, intermediate-size boats for traffic between major towns, and the huge Day Line and Night Line ships between Albany and New York.

When Mother took us on a shopping expedition to Hudson, five miles above Catskill on the other side of the river, we would go on the "Isabella" or the "Robert Livingston." It was a pleasant trip, taking about an hour, and costing ten cents per passenger each way. We usually took the boat from a wharf near Bridge Street in the village of Catskill, so that the trip included a segment on the Catskill Creek past the brick plant and the Hop-O-Nose, a rock formation jutting out in the stream. After Catskill Point we headed north. The steamer would stop at any ice house either on signal of a white cloth waved from shore or at the request of a passenger on board. Regular stops were Hudson, Athens and Catskill. The boats were about 40 feet long and burned coal. There was space to walk around, chairs on the covered deck and a cabin for inclement weather. Young passengers liked to watch activities in the engine room.

Then there were the ferries: the Hudson-Athens and the venerable A.F.Beach making the run between Catskill Point and Greendale, where many New York Central trains stopped for passengers.

Business in my father's drugstore in Athens was best when the Hudson-Athens ferry had shut down for the winter and the river had not frozen sufficiently so that the distance could be walked safely. Fare on the ferry was a dime and the journey took about fifteen minutes. The big excitement was rounding the Athens Lighthouse which still stands at the south end of the long sandy island which divides the river into two channels for a few miles north from Hudson. At times we could see a member of the family living in the lighthouse and almost always we could spot the row boat used in getting back and forth to Hudson or Athens. Automation has now replaced families living in such lighthouses. At one time a canal had been dug across the island so that the ferry could go on a direct route between the two towns, without going around the lighthouse. But the canal silted up and it was not worth while to keep it open. Now that there is a bridge across the river just north of Catskill village, neither ferry is needed.

While I was still in high school my sister and I had a wonderful trip to Albany on the "Ursula," a steamer of intermediate size. We walked to town early in the morning to board the boat at the dock in Catskill Creek. Then after appropriate tootings and unmoorings, the "Ursula" steamed down to Catskill Point and turned north toward Albany 35 miles away. With two or three intermediate stops it took about two hours for the trip. For good viewing we sat on the upper deck. As the river narrows above Hudson, we were always close to shore; trees mostly but occasionally a house or two and a field under cultivation. In Albany there were several hours for Grace and one of her friends who happened to be on the boat to do some shopping and for me to explore a bit. Then we boarded the "Ursula" for the return trip, during which we enjoyed a brilliant sunset.

The Catskill Evening Line had passenger and freight ships running between Catskill Point and New York City. When, as a college student I was a reporter on a Schenectady paper, the city editor told me that the line had the reputation for allowing anyone who paid appropriate fares to occupy cabins. I know nothing about that. The line had two passenger steamers, one leaving Catskill each evening for New York, while the other arrived next morning.

As far as I was concerned it was chiefly a freight line, carrying barrels of fruit to New York City and miscellaneous freight from New York to Catskill. The father of a friend of mine was manager of the freight department and hired me to handle cartons, boxes and barrels

unloaded each day. Apparently I had little aptitude for freight hand-
ling as I lasted on the job only a few days.

The Hudson River Night Line was a major operation, carrying
passengers between New York City and Albany without intermediate
stops. There was much traffic so the huge steamers often traveled in
pairs. As observed a few times when camping near the river, they were
a spectacle of lights as they came up the river at about two o'clock in the
morning. My only direct experience was a few years later when I took
passage in New York as a way of returning to college in Schenectady.
We left fairly late in the evening, there was not much to see from the
deck, and my chief recollection is winning two dollars in the "horse
race," wooden horses advancing according to the throw of the dice.

THE HUDSON RIVER DAY LINE

Ah, the Day Line! The giants, the "Hendrick Hudson" and the
"Washington Irving," were floating palaces with every imaginable extra, lounge chairs indoors and deck chairs outside, space for picnics, a
luxurious dining room with huge windows, an orchestra, and a continuous panoply of views on either side of the river. The smaller boats, such
as the "Albany" and the "Robert Fulton," pretty well met the standards
of the giants.

On the trip north there were two stops in New York City for
loading passengers, then Yonkers, Bear Mountain, Newburgh,
Poughkeepsie, Kingston Point, Catskill, Hudson and Albany. For those
who made the entire trip, it was seven hours or so of spectacular
adventure.

The schedule was such that round trips between New York and
Poughkeepsie, or between Albany and Kingston Point, or any intermediate stop, could be made in a single day. The northbound steamer from
New York was required to land at Poughkeepsie before the southbound
boat from Albany. From Catskill youngsters celebrating birthdays were
often taken on an excursion to Kingston Point for a picnic and a brief
visit to an amusement park. Whenever possible any member of our
family traveling between Catskill and Newburgh used the Hudson
River Day Line, cheaper and far more enjoyable than the train. I used it
for my very memorable first visit to New York and once or twice
between Catskill and Albany.

A family belonging to the Dutch Reformed Church owned the
line and set strict standards: no sailings on Sundays, only classical or
semi-classical music, no gambling of any kind. Sunday sailings began
during World War I, and a few years later ragtime and jazz largely
replaced the classical music of earlier days. When I graduated from

brown bag lunches, I found meals in the restaurant enjoyable for good food, Strauss waltzes and wonderful unfolding scenery.

Despite dozens of families with youngsters that needed watching and admonitions, and tens of picnics in circles of chairs on deck, the steamers were kept remarkably clean by porters on continuous duty. The newsstands were decorous, all personnel were in meticulously clean uniforms and there was nothing resembling the "horse racing" of the Night Line.

The "Washington Irving" was the largest of the Day Line steamers, licensed to carry 6,000 passengers. The "Hendrick Hudson" was older and smaller, but to me both were equally luxurious: floating palaces as far as decoration was concerned, but with practical furniture for passengers. It was a memorable event when the "Washington Irving" made her first voyage up river, and it was a sad day years later when I read of her demise in a freak accident in the Hudson at New York City.

Catskill was one of the most important stops of the Day Line steamers. At the height of the summer session, between one and two thousand passengers would be landed for various destinations in the surrounding resort area and in the mountains. Before World War I there would always be a Catskill Mountain Railroad train waiting to take summer visitors to Cairo or Palenville, or to the junction with the Otis Elevated for transportation to the 2,000 foot level of the mountains. Some of the larger hotels provided stage coaches. After the war, it was a matter of taxis and buses. The taxi drivers, prevented by the police from approaching too close to the passengers, announced destinations by placards and invited patronage with loud voices. In later years my friend Raymond Taylor managed to purchase a Model T Ford and used it to earn money in the summer for his expenses at Cornell. While by no means a raucous individual, Raymond learned how to compete in a tumultuously noisy crowd.

CANOEING

The DuBois family never owned a canoe, nor did any of the families we knew. It is only in recent decades that canoes have become easy to transport on top of a car or on a trailer. After we learned to swim we were permitted to rent canoes at Benter's Boat House on Catskill Creek and paddle to various destinations. Canoeing skill, including steering, was quickly learned, especially since there was very little current in either the creek or the river.

We did not canoe upstream because the creek soon became unnavigable. Often we would paddle down to the Point and from there to various river destinations, a favorite being the Plaatje, a flat sand bar with a tree or two and a name given by early Dutch settlers of the Hudson Valley. Here was a fine place for swimming. Once two of us crossed the river, circumnavigated Roger's Island, north of the Plaatje, and returned to the boat house, a trip of several miles.

There are three small creeks, two flowing into the Catskill, the third directly into the river. The two I knew, DuBois' Creek and Rams-horn Creek, flow through semi-swampy land beloved by wild life. Like the Hudson and the lower part of the Catskill, they are tidal, but only with a foot or two of rise. The two creeks are said to be connected at their headwaters.

Paddling up either was much the same in water that hardly moved. We could see scrawny woods on either side of the stream, bushes, many birds and an occasional animal. One could have a pleasant afternoon on the two-way trip; that is, if nothing interfered. Two friends of mine, Elinor Jennings and Alan Kniffen, paddled up one of the creeks one afternoon and were stranded when the tide went out. A very scratchy walk ensued, particularly harrowing for Elinor who had dressed up for the occasion. It was her first afternoon in heels! Next day Alan took a male companion to retrieve the canoe.

SWIMMING

Swimming was an appropriate summer recreation in Catskill. There were no swimming pools, indoors or outdoors. For years the Hudson was favored for dips, but with general recognition of the unsanitary nature of the river water, most of us chose either the deep water of the lower creek or the fresher water in swimming holes up-stream.

My first swimming lesson was in the river. My sister Grace and one of her friends took me to a home on Hamburg Road, which runs along the river for half a mile. I don't remember where I put on my swim suit but the girls changed in the boathouse into their stockings, sneakers, bloomers, upper garments and bathing caps. In those days, probably 1910 or 1911, women wore lots of clothing when they went into the water. For the swimming lesson I used "water wings," a pair of inflatable bags joined together and sufficiently buoyant so that no effort was needed to stay afloat.

I remember only one "lesson." Thereafter when I went swimming I had water wings available while practicing the breast stroke in shallow water. With that mastered I was ready for swimming off docks, for learning how to tread water and for simple diving, that is, from three to eight feet above water. Eventually a crawl stroke was not too difficult.

When we were at Table Rock or another beach at the river shore, the big event of the morning or afternoon was the Day Line steamer coming by. Someone would shout, "First seeings on the day boat!" In the morning the boat would come by quickly, but in the afternoon it could be seen coming around a bend before landing at Catskill Point to discharge passengers, which sometimes required more than an hour. Finally it would grandly sail by in midchannel. In a few minutes there would be three rollers ("Just like the ocean," Mother said one day when she was at the river shore for a picnic). Then a series of diminishing smaller waves followed. There would be shouts and lots of splashing, but the fun was limited; boat captains were under instructions not to create damaging waves. Again and again we were cautioned against "undertow," which I think was mostly a fiction since the boat was always two or three hundred feet away and posed no hazard to swimmers a little distance from its path.

The big challenge was "swimming the channel," usually from the shore to the Plaatje, a distance of several hundred yards. There was always an accompanying rowboat, and for a reasonably competent swimmer the risk was not great. Friends of mine who accomplished the feat usually did not repeat it—the distinction of having done it was enough.

When we shifted to dock swimming in the lower Catskill Creek, one of my fellow swimmers was a boy a year or so older than I was. He was George H. Decker about to leave Catskill for Lafayette College, where ROTC training led to a distinguished military career climaxed by service as chairman of the Joint Chiefs of Staff. Once when a wet swimmer came near his package of cigarettes, he cautioned, "Be careful, they cost nearly a penny a piece!"

Dock swimming in the creek was fun but the water was only a little cleaner than the river and many of us opted to swim off the rocks at a fine swimming hole upstream. Mostly we walked to swimming places, carrying our swimsuits and sometimes a towel. We would find a place to change, often in the bushes, leave our clothes in a conspicuous place, and change back after swimming and drying off. Afternoon was the favorite time for swimming, although I can remember dips in the morning and occasionally in the evening. As competence increased so did our confidence in swimming in water over our heads. On a hike that took us to Black Lake, Raymond Taylor and I had a dip at a very isolated spot in water of unknown depth. As we had no swimming togs with us, we stripped and cautiously dived from some rocks into the water. Fortunately we encountered no difficulty and, after drying off, resumed our hike of 15 miles or so. Almost always, however, we swam where others were around.

SKATING

In suitable weather skating was important and all the children I knew learned to skate early. There were no rinks, but two very different places for skating: ponds on the one hand and the Hudson River and the Catskill Creek on the other. The three ponds we used exclusively were on the Hopkins property, all comers being welcome. No one, not even members of the Hopkins family, thought that any generosity was involved—it was perfectly natural that everyone could skate on the Hopkins's ponds. All three were safe. If anyone had fallen through the ice on one of the "Little Ponds," which no one ever did, the water would have been less than two feet deep. The "Big Pond" was three or four feet deeper. Here the ice broke a time or two but without serious results.

I well remember my first attempt to skate. Some of my young friends had twin-bladed training skates that enabled them to stand on the ice and presumably helped them to develop skill, although the matter is debatable. Anyway I was presented at Christmas with single bladed skates. I was probably seven at the time. My sister took me over to one of the little ponds which were not far from The Ridge, and helped me attach the skates to my shoes. I was unaware of the hazards. The big boys and girls seemed to be moving effortlessly, so I got up and started off. The first stroke was a disaster. I tumbled, falling backward. There was laughter. I was comforted and given instruction. Very awkwardly I tried again and succeeded in standing upright on my skates and taking a stroke or two. In a couple of sessions I gained enough skill to enjoy "going skating."

As a group Catskill skaters were satisfied with a low level of proficiency: straight-a-way at low speed, some backward skill, and hand-to-hand skating in pairs. The bigger boys played a rudimentary version of hockey, involving two teams, a puck, hockey sticks and goals marked on the ice. There was much activity and much shouting, but the game was seldom sufficiently organized to count score.

With a cold snap before a snowfall, the ponds were reasonably satisfactory but they were small and often crowded. Ice was harvested both in Catskill Creek and in the river. It was not possible to skate on either before the harvest because of preparations while the ice was still thin. After the harvest was in and if there had been no snow, the fields would freeze smooth and once in a while provide excellent skating. All this was before artificial ice replaced natural ice in New York City and ice breakers were introduced on the Hudson to keep the river open for navigation all year.

An older skater I remember well was a West Pointer, a Major Beach, who had retired from the Army before World War I and had greatly increased the proportion of West Pointers retiring as colonels and generals. He enjoyed both skating and being with youngsters. It was he who showed me how to make figure 8's, my highest skating accomplishment.

In the course of a winter we usually found opportunity to skate several times, with pleasant exercise both in the skating and walking back and forth in the crisp air. As time went on, most of us graduated from skates that were attached to shoes as we now have today.

I continued to skate through college days, and when I returned to the United States after three years in the semi-tropics, I tried skating again, apparently with no loss of skill.

SNOW AND ICE

While I lived in Catskill there was snow in November only once or twice. However, there was lots of snow in December, with white Christmases the rule rather than the exception.

Deep snow involved a chore. Harry and I would dig a long path from the house down the hill to the highway. When the snow was deep and the temperature low, the work was fatiguing. Nowadays Jake contracts with a service company to open up his access road whenever there is more than a light snow, so that the chore of shoveling snow is pretty well a thing of the past.

We had lots of fun in the snow. Jake and I made ourselves snow shoes from barrel staves, but they had utility only in demonstrating how deep snow could be traversed. Skiing was more to the point—our skis came from Mike Cimorelli's store, and we had some success in skiing the hilly cow pastures near The Ridge. No lifts, no tickets, no steep slopes, no ski instructors. We walked to the top of the hill, sometimes awkwardly on skis, and then swooshed down, the only hazzard being a possible dunking in a snow bank.

When the temperature was a bit above freezing we did what even city kids could do—we made a snow man. Attempts at igloo building were not very successful, but a well-made snow fort occasionally provided just the right location for an exciting snowball fight.

When snowfall was heavy so that snow could be harvested without dirt, Mother sometimes helped us make "snow ice cream," newly fallen snow enhanced with sugar and vanilla flavoring. More often, we would get out the freezer, while she prepared real ice cream with proper ingredients. Then it would be our job to pack salt and snow around the cylinder and turn the crank until delicious ice cream resulted. This was also a summer event, with ice brought from town instead of snow gathered from the lawn.

AN EXPANDING WORLD

BOY SCOUT ACTIVITIES

TWICE I was involved in an attempt to start a club. Once Edward Jones, George Bagley, George Van Tine and I organized what we called The Book Club. The idea was to lend each other books. It did not last long despite a constitution modeled after that of the United States.

The Camp Club lasted a little longer. There were requirements for several levels of membership, just as in the Boy Scouts. In fact, the Boy Scout handbook was the inspiration and model for the organization. It was decided that Bobby Tompkins did not meet standards and therefore could not join; an unwise decision that irritated his aunts with whom he lived. Then Edward Jones decided to withdraw and form the Order of Electrical Engineers. All this led me to a middle of the night decision when I pounded my pillow and resolved to join a real life organization, the Boy Scouts.

I discovered that Troop 1, the only Boy Scout troop in Catskill, met in the Parish House of the Episcopal Church. I showed up one night and told the scoutmaster, Mr. Ted Hall, son of the owner of *The Recorder*, the leading weekly newspaper, that I wanted to join. Using the Boy Scout handbook, I already had prepared for the tenderfoot examination and, right on the spot, passed it without difficulty. It was the spring of 1916, a few months before my 13th birthday. For the next five years I was an enthusiastic and active scout (and later, when I was in college, I participated in summers as an assistant scoutmaster).

After I joined the troop we met only a few times in the Parish House. Apparently there had been some roughhousing—an official of the church appeared one night and told us what we would have to do in order to continue our meetings there. Mr. Hall, a member of the church, was angry at conditions he considered unnecessary, and we voted to leave. For a time we met in a Sunday School room of the Dutch Reformed Church, and then at the YMCA, which became a more or less permanent meeting place.

As a Boy Scout I advanced quickly. I remember thinking that the promotion to second class scout was a real achievement. Then came fulfilling the requirements for first class rank and for a modest collection of merit badges—but not those required for Life, Star or Eagle Scout. At that time a merit badge in athletics was a basic requirement, and to me that seemed unattainable. However, I had my uniform, interest continued, and I rode my bike back and forth to the evening meetings.

American involvement in World War I came during my second year as a Scout, and then there were parades and parades. The Boy Scouts were called upon to march in every parade in town—chiefly in connection with Liberty Loan drives—but at the end of the war there was the parade celebrating what turned out to be a false report of an armistice, then the real armistice celebration, a Victory Liberty Loan drive, and a welcome home for the 27th Division, formed from the New York State National Guard. Scouts were not supposed to be military, but we had khaki uniforms and marched well—at least we thought so!

One time during the war some local Italians gave an opera—*Il Trovatore*—at the Nelida Theater. A tenor was imported from New York. Two Scouts, of which I was one, were invited to appear on the stage with him as he sang a patriotic song during intermission. The song referred to a soldier on the right and a soldier on the left—our job was merely to stand in the assigned spots. During the rehearsal it was a new experience to hear local residents chatting with the visitor in a foreign language. *Il Trovatore* was my first opera, and the part I liked best was the "Anvil chorus."

While the war was at its height, Mr. Hall thought his troop should have a garden. He obtained permission to use a large lot on Hamburg Road and persuaded someone to plow it. When he didn't get enough volunteers to work the plot he prescribed a minimum amount of time each Scout should work there each week. Some of us did put in some hours trying to soften up the hard soil, but as far as I know, nothing was ever planted.

Another wartime project was to canvass homes to persuade people to sign promises to buy Thrift Stamps and Liberty Bonds. I canvassed all the houses in Hamburg, the stretched-out settlement along the river. I got more arguments than signatures. One oldster, whom I learned many years later was the grandfather of a classmate, told me that "they," meaning the government, were conscripting the wrong people. "They should get men like me. I'm tough—I can take it," he said. I said something about decisions made by experts in Washington. He had nothing good to say about experts in Washington. "What do they know?"

The easiest wartime assignment was distributing a government pamphlet prepared by George Creel and his propaganda organization. It contained President Wilson's Flag Day speech and the Fourteen Points he proposed as the basis for peace. (Eight or ten years later I learned from Bayard Dodge, president of the American University of Beirut, that those Fourteen Points had been written out at the Dodge family home in Riverdale, N.Y.) I never read the pamphlet all the way through, but I did take it to all the houses in my assigned territory, again Hamburg, and collected signatures.

GEORGE PARK, SCOUTMASTER

We did some hiking with Mr. Hall, but a Mr. George Park volunteered to be an assistant Scoutmaster to take the boys on bicycle trips. Mr. Park was a printer who had recently brought his family to town. It included two sons, who became very active Scouts.

Twice Mr. Park took us to the summit of Slide Mountain where we camped for the night. Slide, at 4,180 feet, is the highest mountain in the Catskills. The trip involved 50 miles of bicycling each way and several miles of hiking. The climb is not difficult as there is a good trail to the top. We would leave our bicycles in Big Indian with a kind individual who did not mind custody of a dozen or more bicycles while we climbed the mountain. The trail was mostly in the woods, but there were some views of interest, particularly of Wittenberg Mountain, not as high as Slide but less accessible. At the summit we made camp. We had to carry both food and water up the mountain. For meals on a bicycle trip Mr. Park declared that bacon and flapjacks were enough—a horrible idea to Mother who insisted that we carry more conventional food, including fruit. My brother and I had to withstand some social pressure on the subject of camp food but Mother won out.

After a long day of cycling and climbing, supper around the campfire was wonderful. A mountaintop stimulates conversation, and we were tired enough to get lots of sleep despite the clear sky, wondrous stars overhead and the invisible porcupines squealing nearby. All would wake up early in the morning to fix some breakfast, pack and get ready to take the trail back to Big Indian and the road back to Catskill.

Mr. Park loved the out of doors and communed with mountains, lakes and forests. He knew the geography of the southern Catskills, the names of the peaks and the configurations of the streams. He was encouraging when the route seemed long and we youngsters became fatigued. His planning was such that all expeditions were well within our capacities. He set a good pace while cycling—not too fast for the slower boys and not too slow for those who liked to speed.

One of our best excursions was to Lake Awosting in the Shawangunk Mountains, west of New Paltz. One of the lakes in the area is Lake Mohonk with a large and famous resort hotel. Awosting was on undeveloped private property, and somehow Mr. Park had secured permission to camp there for a couple of nights. Again a long bicycle ride was involved but now there was a quiet campsite along a beautiful lake, with the light of the fire reflected in the water.

I never discovered how much formal education Mr. Park had but like many printers of the time he must have been largely self-taught. He owned a New Testament with parallel Greek and Latin texts, which he said he read every night. He told of reading Dante, but admitted that the Italian presented some difficulties. He knew great literature, and I remember particularly his discussions of Browning. He did not flaunt learning but would carry a conversation to any depth a boy wanted. He confided he had written a novel and I spent a day reading the typescript. I liked it but I do not know what effort he made to have it published. After I returned from Lebanon I lent him a couple of books in French I had bought in Moscow, including Lenin's "L'Etat et la Revolution." He read them with interest, as works that broadened his point of view.

I look back at my years as a Boy Scout as 100 percent constructive. Both scoutmasters were clean in thought and were good examples but in very different ways. Mr. Hall was matter-of-fact and constantly serious; Mr. Park was fun-loving, extroverted and possessed of a wide range of interests. Both provided wholesome contacts with grownups.

The requirement for grades and merit badges helped to establish goals at an appropriate level of endeavor. The weekly meetings included a bit of drill, plans for forthcoming activities, and perhaps a special feature, such as a friendly contest of some sort. However, much of the content of scouting came from the interesting and informative Boy Scout handbook and from *Boys' Life*, a monthly magazine which I read regularly.

MY BIKE

When it was decided that I was old enough to have a bicycle, Dad ordered one for me. I said I did not need mud guards, so they were not included in the order. For rainy days this turned out to be a mistake because of the splatter from the front wheel. However, on long trips in good weather the lighter weight was a definite advantage.

One day while expecting the bike to arrive I happened to see one crated in the Express Office. Excitedly I popped in and asked, "Do you have a bicycle for Philip DuBois?" "No," was the reply, "We have a bicycle for so and so." A big disappointment, but the bike finally arrived—by freight. It had a good coaster brake and a bell, but no light for night riding.

While expecting it, I learned to ride on Grace's girl-style bicycle. First I practiced on the front lawn until I could ride fairly well. Then I set forth on Grace's bike to go to Athens four miles away, where at that time Dad owned a drugstore. It was an adventure. The road was dusty and the day was sunny. I was cautious of automobiles coming from either direction so I dismounted as soon as I heard or saw one. On the hills I rode only when the grade was not too steep.

I made it all right. My father was glad to see me. He ate my lunch with Mother's homemade bread and I ate his with store bread. It was a good exchange for both. Then I went home the same way. I didn't make much speed, but I gained confidence and when my bike actually arrived I could ride it to school and to Boy Scout meetings in the evenings and eventually on long trips.

After Dad sold the Athens store and bought Uncle Arthur's store in Newburgh, I rode down there at least twice. The paved 60-mile route took me through New Paltz, ancestral home of the New York State DuBois family. On a mail box I noticed the name of Philip H. DuBois but I was too shy to go to the door and introduce myself as another Philip H. DuBois. I later discovered he was a fruit grower and a solid citizen. Each time I stayed two or three nights in Newburgh. With the young man who was helping Dad in his store, I revisited Downing Park and took the funicular up Mount Beacon across the river. Dad wanted me to take the Day Boat back to Catskill, and I did not object.

HIKING

During high school my chief hiking companions were Edward Jones and Raymond Taylor. Both were good hikers and good talkers. Sometimes we used bicycles to get into position for a ramble or a climb.

Edward and I explored the Cauterskill Cave in the Kalkberg range, between Catskill and the mountains. Its entrance is so small that we had to squeeze to enter. We found the inside much larger but with little to see. Then there was Vedder Hill in much the same formation and clearly visible from The Ridge. It has a magnificent view east toward the river. Raymond and I rode out there several times to climb the hill or to chat with a classmate, Mary Vedder, whose family farm was at the base. Cairo-Roundtop, a stand-alone mini-mountain, was once a destination for a pleasant ramble. On an overnight bicycle trip several of us rode out to the northern part of the Catskill range and climbed part way up Black Head, an uninhabited mountain with a forbidding appearance. The camping was fun despite a bit of rain in the middle of the night.

Raymond and I liked to hike up Vosenkill Road, named for the small stream which flows parallel not far away, and then up on the northern Kalkberg, perhaps to Black Lake, picturesque and isolated. Once I took the same route alone with a copy of Ruskin's essays in my pocket to read while resting. Sometimes rambles took us to the river shore where the flow of ice cakes in the spring was an arresting sight.

Again and again we spent time in Austin's Glen, where the Catskill Creek cuts though many geological layers and where water, rocks and trees make beautiful scenes. It was here that Prof. George H. Chadwick, who grew up in Catskill and was then teaching geology at the University of Rochester, would bring his students on a field trip to inspect what he said was a greater variety of waterlaid rock than could be observed anywhere else in the eastern United States. I was present at one of his campfires when he asked two of his colleagues to tell of their travel experiences. One described a visit to Spitzbergen, another a trip to the Dead Sea. Immediately I developed an ambition to go to both places. About eight years later I did have a swim in the Dead Sea, but eventually I lost ambition to visit Spitzbergen.

The roadbed of the Catskill Mountain Railroad offered a good way to hike through the glen and on to the third bridge, not far from Cairo. Here Raymond Taylor liked to demonstrate his sang-froid by climbing high up on the girders where no one would attempt to follow. He was agile, sure-footed and confident, but his exploits produced shivers in his companions.

The glen was a good place for hiking in all seasons, winter, summer, and in between. It was also a good place for photography, and some of my earliest attempts at taking landscapes were in Austin's Glen.

Hiking often involved carrying a lunch, which Mother prepared with care: typically, a couple of sandwiches with sliced meat, jelly or peanut butter; a hardboiled egg with a packet of salt; and whatever fruit was available. Even when I was old enough to prepare my own lunch, she supervised the contents. Always the appetites of hikers tend to be excellent!

THE OTHER SIDE OF THE RIVER

Almost all of our hiking was on the west side of the Hudson, as interesting destinations were numerous and attractive. However two or three of us decided to visit an abandoned iron mine we had heard about, a few miles south of the Greendale Station. It was a simple matter to take the ferry from Catskill Point and then hike along the railroad tracks to the mine. There was little to see except a yawning opening and we saw no reason to attempt a deep penetration. The mine did not seem to have been profitably productive. Here and there in this part of New York State are traces of mineralization, but commercial mining has been directed chiefly to limestone for making cement.

Almost exactly across from The Ridge (but not visible from it because of intervening hills) is a building high up on the east shore of the river which we knew as "Church's Castle." It is surrounded by trees and stands out whenever one looks across the river from any spot along Catskill's river shore. It seemed like an appropriate goal for a hike, so several of us took the ferry and rambled through the woods and up the steep hill until "Church's Castle" loomed up just above us. Whether Frederick Church's daughter would have welcomed us, we never discovered—we were too timid to find out. At that time we did not know that "Church's Castle" was better known as Olana.

Years later I visited Olana after it became a fine state museum with truly wonderful views up and down the Hudson and across to the Catskills. It includes a collection of Church's paintings in the magnificent home in which he lived and worked. In recent years whenever I see one of his landscapes, I remember my two visits to Olana.

AUTOMOBILES

I do not remember when I first saw an automobile (undoubtedly in Newburgh) or took my first auto ride (certainly in Catskill), but I do remember when cars were still curiosities. There was some sort of a long distance automobile race—probably Albany to New York—about 1910, and people waited along the road to see the cars. About the same time Marion Blodgett visited us and told about her automobile ride: "We went a mile in four minutes! That's some traveling!"

When we moved to Catskill, the road to Athens was dirt. Some time later it was paved, and I heard that it would be an asphalt road. I asked the operator of the steam roller the color of asphalt. "Black," he said, "but after it is covered with crushed stone, the road looks white."

The paved road and the introduction of automobiles changed our habits, as might be expected. Before then, as a special treat, Dad took us once in a while in a hired surrey with a fringe on top for long drives in the country. The back roads may have been dusty, and the day may have been hot, but the trips were always adventures: up and down hills, panoramic views, and here and there a farm house with cows, horses and chickens. When it became possible to hire an open touring car with a driver, the speed was faster and we went further from The Ridge, but the occasions were really no more enjoyable.

Gradually autos became commonplace, especially Model T's. A friend of the family, who dealt in grain and cars, went bankrupt. He said that people all over the county owed him money on their cars. Apparently he had extended credit in the old fashioned way he had used in the grain business—no security, just a promise to pay. With cars that wasn't enough. A little later car manufacturers and car dealers developed better methods of insuring payment.

AIRPLANES

I was born almost exactly five months before the Wright brothers made their first airplane flights, with the result that, when I began to read newspapers, many stories had to do with aircraft: the first flight in the rain; night flights; a flight carrying a passenger, with photographs and a graphic map; and speculations on how aircraft might be used in a war. Frank Wilcoxson, one of Shorty's friends, told how his father had arranged for a flight but made the mistake of walking out to the wrong plane. He argued so long with the pilot that the plane that was supposed to take him had taken off. No airlines in those days, no tickets, just planes using flat fields.

When Glenn Martin, an aviation pioneer whose fame is perpetuated in the name of the Martin Marietta Corporation, flew down the Hudson Valley in stages, Dad alerted us by way of the Kerr telephone. Mother decided we should watch from the top of the Pine Lot. The Hopkins boys went by, saying they were going over to the river shore and invited us to go along. Mother said no. When the plane actually came by, it flew so low that it was obscured by the wooded hill east of The Ridge. Harry and I were back in the house during the crucial minutes; Mother heard the motor but saw nothing. Later the Hopkins boys reported they had had a good view. We were disappointed. Later Dad gave us a photo taken from Athens, on which the plane seemed very, very tiny.

A few years later, in 1918, I had my first view of an airplane. Katherine Stinson was making a flight in support of a Liberty Loan Drive. Aunt Hattie and I had walked to Cousin Till's a dozen miles northwest of The Ridge for an overnight visit. We saw the Stinson plane flying nicely. Then black smoke emerged, the plane made a U-turn and descended. We later learned that Miss Stinson landed safely in a field and eventually resumed her flight.

Later a plane flew over Catskill dropping leaflets urging the purchase of Liberty Bonds. I retrieved a copy and kept it—a piece of paper that had actually been up in an airplane! Soon airplanes became a fairly common sight. The time of the mail plane between Albany and New York was fairly predictable. Then a young man we knew slightly bought an old biplane and flew it around in early evening when winds are low. One time he circled around The Ridge, evidently knowing it as our house. Then a West Point flight trainee named Anderson got into the habit of buzzing Catskill because he had a girl friend living there. She eventually became Mrs. Anderson and in World War II he went on to become General Anderson.

My own first flight came years later. For the experience I flew as a passenger in a Lufthansa plane from Nuremberg to Munich in 1926. The pilot and the luggage were up front and the four passengers were in the cabin of a metal monoplane. It was still pioneering!

THE STORY FAMILY

Grace Donohue and my Mother, Hattie Aletha Clough, were close friends as they grew up in Catskill. They agreed that each would name their first born girl after the other. When a baby girl was born to Grace Donohue Story and John H. Story, she was named Aletha and when the second child of Hattie Aletha Clough DuBois turned out to be a girl, she was named Grace.

After the DuBois family moved from Newburgh to Catskill, the fact that Dad and John Story were both descendants of a French Huguenot, Louis DuBois, who settled in the Hudson Valley in the seventeenth century, cemented relationships between the families. The Storys lived on New Street, which intersects Thompson Street right at Irving School. The older Story son, Bob, became one of Shorty's companions. Grace and Aletha knew each other well, and the two families had many social contacts, reinforced by membership in the Dutch Reformed Church. We youngsters always knew Mrs. Story as "Aunt Grace" and Mr. Story as "Uncle John." At Sunday School, I discovered that Aunt Grace was a privileged person—as organist she could keep her eyes open during prayers!

When I was in the fourth grade at Irving School, my classmate, Bill Donohue, and I were looking out of my window toward New Street. I spotted Mr. Story. "There goes my Uncle John," I said. "That's MY Uncle John!" said Bill. And so it really was, since Bill was the son of Grace Donohue Story's brother.

John Story had three sisters living in Catskill: Sarah, always called Sally; Mary; and Martha, always called Mattie. We called all three cousins. With their brother they shared a mother who had been born a DuBois, and Cousin Sally seemed especially interested in DuBois family

history. She borrowed Dad's copy of the "DuBois Book," which my
Grandfather Anson had prepared, and helped preserve the volume by
adding a protective cover. Late in life she called my brother Harry, and
told him she would endow the DuBois family cemetery in West Catskill
if he would agree to be a trustee. He agreed, and for many years the
cemetery has been kept in good shape. When I returned in 1928 from
three years in Lebanon, Grace thought that Cousin Sally would have lots
of questions about my experiences abroad. But Cousin Sally was 70 at
the time, lived quietly and comfortably with few contacts outside her
house, and soon showed she had other things to talk about. Grace was
disappointed.

Cousin Mattie was married to a local shoe merchant. They had no
children. In the Dutch church, most of the pews were rented, and hers
was across the aisle from ours and one or two back. Accordingly, we
saw her almost every Sunday. She arrived a few minutes early, dressed
to perfection, walking sedately and seating herself with careful dignity.

Mary, whom we called Cousin Mame, was the most sociable of
the three. Like Cousin Sally, she was unmarried but she was far more a
part of the world. She taught school for many years and built for herself
and her guests a vacation lodge on a mountain ledge up above Palenville.
Some years after she died Margaret Eloise and I received a fine braided
rag rug, delivered in accordance with her instructions, as a posthumous
wedding gift.

THIRTEEN CHRISTMASES AT THE RIDGE

I lived at The Ridge for 13 Christmases, 1908 through 1920. While
I was in college, there were four more Christmases at home, 1921
through 1924. When I was in Lebanon from 1925 to 1928, I was homesick
only at Christmas time, despite wonderful parcels from home and kind
invitations from Beirut families. Then came five years in New York,
when again I was able to be at The Ridge at Christmas. It is not possible
to describe the 13 boyhood Christmases individually or chronologically.
All Christmases were managed chiefly by Mother, later with Grace as a
principal helper. A tree was central, sometimes cut on our property,
more often on a property of a neighbor who was never known to object.
Sometimes it was a white pine, often a hemlock and very occasionally a
spruce. It was always decorated on Christmas Eve. There were a few
glass colored balls dating from Newburgh days, strings of tinsel and an
angel at the top of the tree. These were the decorations that had been
purchased years before. We always strung yards of popcorn, and sometimes made loops of colored paper into garlands. Candles were deemed

too dangerous and there was no electricity for light bulbs, but every tree was a beautiful sight!

Although there was no fireplace at The Ridge, there was a mantel in the parlor where we youngsters hung our stockings, real life stockings but carefully washed for the occasion. It was a fixed rule that packages underneath the tree in the parlor could not be opened or even closely inspected before the family assembled before breakfast, but that stockings could be taken upstairs as early as one wanted. Harry and I usually crept downstairs together to see the tree and take our stockings back upstairs to bed.

In the toe was always an orange, and above that other things to eat: carefully wrapped figs, stuffed dates and homemade Christmas candy, generally a white fudge topped with half an English walnut. Then nuts in shells—Brazil nuts, almonds, English walnuts and filberts which we called hazel nuts. While some of the goodies were consumed immediately, there was always much remaining for later on.

For the formal Christmas we had dressed and we went into the parlor together. Dad presided and distributed the packages. Once Shorty dressed up as Santa Claus, but Harry and I penetrated his disguise and didn't play up to him. He was disappointed but he continued to play the part until all gifts had been distributed.

Givers of presents were identified by appropriate inscriptions, but some were officially from Santa Claus even though we knew he wasn't real. Incidentally, we were instructed to be circumspect about the existence of Santa Claus when we played with Pell Hopkins. At the Hopkins house a glass of cherry bounce was left on the mantel over the fireplace every Christmas eve and every Christmas morning it was gone. "That," said Pell, "proves there is a Santa Claus!" Obviously, the proof was fabricated by his parents. I assume that "bounce" is some sort of a wine; I haven't encountered the word elsewhere.

Usually Harry and I had no advance information about Christmas presents, as they were typically very well hidden, but one Christmas Eve after we had gone to bed and were presumed to be asleep, we saw Grace and Mother go to a clothes closet in the room, and take out from a high storage area some boxes which eventually were found under the tree.

Two presents I particularly remember, both wonderful surprises. One was a movie projector with some film. Today it would be considered exceedingly crude, but it provided some jerky motion and I had a motion picture machine! The other was an Indian suit, complete with fringe and a feathered headdress. Harry's present was similar. The headdresses did not last very long but the Indian suits were worn many,

many days as we played around The Ridge and in the Pine Lot. Year after year gifts included toys and games, such as parcheesi, and books as we became able to read them.

At The Ridge oatmeal was a favorite breakfast food and Hornby's, made in Buffalo, was the favorite brand. The abbreviation was H.O. and in each box was a coupon. I saved enough coupons to send for a tiny electric engine, powered by a dry cell. It apparently arrived just before Christmas, since I found it under the Christmas tree with the inscription, "Philip from Mr. H.O."

Opening the presents and playing with them kept us busy most of Christmas, with durable acquisitions that lasted for months. We always had the feeling of being treated generously and I can recall no feeling of envy when seeing more lavish arrays of gifts in other households.

The house was always decorated for Christmas with greens from the Pine Lot made into garlands and, for the windows, wreaths with red ribbons. And at church the sanctuary was always well decorated, the carols wonderful, and the reading of the Christmas story enthralling. Winifred Fiero, a family friend, was the organist, and I thought her Christmas carols were the most beautiful music imaginable. And in the main Sunday School room there would be an enormous Christmas tree, with a present for each child, who would come forward as the name was called.

For many Christmas seasons a chief event was the arrival of a box from our California relatives, Mother's sister Aunt Ella, her husband Jim and their two sons, James and Frederic. The box arrived with Wells Fargo Express markings, a flavor of the Old West. It was filled with oranges and nuts and dried fruits that gave the impression of California plenty. Many years later when I visited the Tolley family in Orland I discovered that their "ranch" consisted of very few acres and was not nearly as productive as we had imagined. The box had required kind thought and effort.

THE TITANIC

The White Star liner "Titanic" sank in the Atlantic in the early morning of April 15, 1912. It was probably late afternoon on the following day that Shorty brought to The Ridge a copy of *The New York World* with our first news of the disaster. A huge spread across the top of the front page depicted the ship and the accompanying story gave the facts known at the time, including survivors and passengers presumed drowned.

At the time I was about to complete third grade. I recall no difficulty in reading the newspaper account, which not only reported the event but also introduced concepts of which third grade geography had given only hints: huge steamships carrying passengers and cargo across some three thousand miles of ocean; icebergs with which those steamships might collide; the law of the sea during dire emergencies— women and children first to enter lifeboats; and water two miles deep.

Of course the grownups, Mother, Shorty and Grace, were sources of information as well as the newspaper. They, of course, had acquired quite a bit of information about oceans and ships, but it was a startling event that resulted in quite a lot of learning, together with several ideas that eventually proved false. Somehow I thought the vessel would hold together as it plunged toward the bottom, that it might be possible to raise it intact, and that the water was so cold that bodies would be preserved. When the wreck was actually visited more than seventy-five years after the sinking, the truth turned out to be quite different.

News of the sinking reached New York through a fairly new invention, the wireless telegraph. It was soon widespread knowledge that wireless had been used to warn personnel on the "Titanic" of icebergs in her path and that as the ship was sinking wireless had been used to summon help. Interest in wireless accelerated and soon Pell Hopkins had a wireless receiving set, purchased from the Radio Corporation of America founded by David Sarnoff, the wireless operator who at the time of the disaster had received messages from various ships and had relayed the reports. Pell would put on his headphones and listen for many minutes at a time but his success was limited to hearing time signals and an occasional bit of unintelligible code.

RADIO

When I left The Ridge for college in 1921, radio broadcasting was just beginning. In just a year or two there were enough stations on the air so that it became worthwhile to have a set—so one was purchased for The Ridge. I think that Jake took the initiative in acquiring an instrument with earphones. The headset could be divided so that two persons could listen simultaneously. After he retired in 1924, Dad liked to check the current quotation for AT&T, his chief stock investment, on the daily broadcast from WGY in Schenectady. Mother was not enthusiastic about earphones.

In the early 1930's, when I was repaying Dad some money which he had kindly lent me for graduate school expenses, I suggested that he might like, in part payment, a radio which needed no earphones but could be heard throughout the room. He agreed, and thereafter Dad and Mother had much enjoyment from the programs of the day—concerts,

"Amos and Andy," and much, much more. The development coincided with other bits of modernization at The Ridge, chiefly electricity made possible at long last by an electric line along the Athens Road and a telephone.

HOW WORLD WAR I CAME TO THE RIDGE

When World War I began in August, 1914, it seemed very remote from Catskill. *The Knickerbocker Press* was, of course, full of war news, some of which I read but with limited understanding of what was going on. I remember awaiting news of the fall of Paris, but that was averted by the Battle of the Marne, and then came months and months and months of bloody trench warfare. Soon we had books, Empey's *Over the Top* and the memoirs of Private Peat, but neither the books nor the daily papers nor the pictures in the rotogravure section of the Sunday *New York Times* conveyed the unrelenting horror of a war that went on and on with only a few triumphs on either side.

At The Ridge the chief sources of information about the steps toward American involvement were the newspapers in which we read about the sinking of the "Lusitania" by a German submarine, the subsequent protests of the United States, and the German declaration of unrestricted submarine warfare. Finally various considerations resulted in President Wilson's call for war with Germany.

Like the rest of the country, Catskill was soon deeply involved. Its National Guard unit was called to active duty, its young men were required to register for the draft; some enlisted, others waited until their number was reached. It was many months before any appreciable number of local names appeared on casualty lists but there was apprehension from the start. At The Ridge we put out a flag signifying that Shorty was in service: a blue star in a white field surrounded by a red border. Between his training at Fort Benjamin Harrison and his going overseas to France, Shorty spent a few days at The Ridge. He explained to Mother the reason for his choice of the Field Artillery: "If I get it, it will be all at once—I won't be coming home with an arm or a leg missing." I don't believe Mother found this or any other aspect of his military service attractive. She was somewhat reassured with Shorty's belief that he was being sent to a French school for training in the work of a field artillery officer and that he would soon be back in the United States as an instructor. He entered training at Saumur in the Loire Valley, but, instead of service at home at the conclusion of training, he was assigned to 131st Field Artillery, a Minnesota National Guard outfit newly arrived from America and in need of officers trained in the use of the French 75mm field gun. The 131st was a part of the Rainbow Division, formed of units from many states. In his self-censored letters, Shorty revealed nothing of his activities or his whereabouts until, greatly to our relief, the fighting ceased and his outfit went to the Rhineland with the occupation troops.

On the American home front in World War I, civilian life was not greatly changed. The rationing of sugar was little more than a nuisance. At the time Grace was living in a Columbia University dormitory and reported that the girls saved their little envelopes of sugar doled out for their coffee so that they could make fudge! In Catskill I cannot remember being affected by any shortages.

There were many drives—to sell war bonds and thrift stamps, to collect scrap metal, and to save and turn in peach pits at designated collection points. It was officially stated that charcoal from peach pits was needed for gas masks. From the first Dad said that the idea of the drive was to make the Germans believe that the Americans were preparing to use prussic acid in gas warfare. As it turned out the peach pits weren't used for anything except for the ploy that Dad had discerned. I seem to remember that a few women from Catskill had active duty with the Red Cross on the war front but that many were recruited for Red Cross activities at home.

As the war continued, more and more Catskill young men were drafted for Army service, and eventually there were reports of casualties. Fortunately, the Armistice came before the proportion of losses approached those of the European countries. Catskill welcomed her soldiers home—and the storm was over.

SPECIAL OCCASIONS

SUNDAY SCHOOL

W HEN old enough, Harry and I went to Sunday School regularly, walking the distance of one mile down Spring Street to Bridge
Street, and then down the hill by one of several streets to the Sunday
School door. Rudolph Plush was the superintendent who seemed to
manage everything. I remember him taking me to a classroom new to
me and saying that I would be there four years. Four years seemed like
a small eternity, but it was only because grades three through six met in
different corners of the same room.

We had songs, prayers, Bible stories to hear and Bible verses to
learn. Dad thought that a leaflet I brought home with a picture of the
Garden of Eden included impossible details. Elinor Jennings with her
long curls was in the same room but after a while her family transferred
to a different church and I saw her infrequently until dancing class and
high school.

One year the Sunday School celebrated its ancestry with a Dutch
festival, with blue and orange decorations and with some of the girls in
Dutch costumes. For many years our minister was Rev. John A. Dykstra,
young, pleasant, and greatly missed when he left for another pastorate.

When the four years were finally up, I attended a class on the
main floor and, in due time, was promoted to the Young Men's Bible
Class, meeting in the pastor's study, and taught by August Franz, our
first male teacher.

After Sunday School we attended church, where Mother would
be waiting for us in Pew #103. In the Dutch church it was the custom to
put one's head on the rail of the pew in front as soon as seated and pray

silently. As I heard later, we prayed on our foreheads—at the time it seemed perfectly natural.

In the winter of 1914-15 an evangelist came to the church and made a powerful plea for Christianity. He asked everyone to sign a card having to do with the acceptance of Christian principles. Along with most everybody in the upper grades of the Sunday School, I signed the card. Then, to the surprise of all of us, we learned that the cards were considered applications for membership in the church. On a certain Sunday over a hundred of us were lined up in the front of the church and taken into membership. The pastor told of certain saints who had joined the early church before the age of 12. I certainly was not a saint, but in the spring of 1915 I was only 11. For the minister it was a great occasion—I still think there was a lack of candor in the proceedings. However, as long as I lived in Catskill I attended church more or less regularly, and joined my family there when I was home from college.

SUNDAY SCHOOL PICNICS

The big event of the Sunday School year was the picnic, always in a pine grove in Palenville at the foot of the mountains, and always, until it ceased operations, involving a wonderful trip on the Catskill Mountain Railroad. Trains that met Day Line steamers started from Catskill Point, but picnic excursion trains started at creekside in town, just outside the railroad office. Edward Jones' uncle, Tom Jones, who managed the railroad, was generally to be seen assuring himself that everything was in order. I didn't know the engineer of the old-fashioned steam locomotive, but it was likely to have been Mike Cimorelli whom I knew quite well later. Mike saved his money, was able to buy Cooper's run down bicycle shop, enlarged its scope to handle many sorts of sports equipment including motorcycles, and eventually became one of Catskill's most prosperous and respected citizens.

At the appointed hour, we would all gather alongside the train. Rudy Plush would hand everyone a ticket as we waited for the "all aboard" signal. At the appropriate time we would climb into the tiny cars on the narrow gauge track, two children to a seat. The engine would toot, the younger kids would squeal and off we'd go: along the creek, and past the foundry and across the creek on the first bridge. The train would travel along the creek to the second bridge just before Rushmore's dam, then a couple of miles through Austin's Glen to the third bridge. Next it would traverse a bit of open country to a right-of-way along the road leading to Cairo. Finally it would make a long curve to the south past Lawrenceville and Otis Junction to Palenville. Sometime along the way there would be a great event: the conductor coming by to lift the first half of the ticket. We read the warning posted by each window: Passengers must not put head or arms outside windows. Just east of the mountain face, the railroad route was in somewhat flat country from which the mountain loomed up to what seemed a great height. This was all the more astonishing because we had much the same view from The Ridge, but on a much reduced scale because of the intervening miles.

Once we were in Palenville we would walk a few hundred yards south to the picnic grove, with no underbrush below the pines which sheltered a number of tables and benches. The grove had a wonderful woodsy smell.

For the picnic everything was well organized. The meal came first, served on paper plates. The DuBois children were under strict instructions from Mother not to eat pickles or mustard. There were potato chips, probably frankfurters, and certainly lemonade and ice cream. After the meal was over and plates and napkins had been put in the barrels, there were games. There was usually an excursion up the mountain on the Otis cable railway. This cost money—fifty cents— much less than the fare paid by travelers. I took the trip once, a never-to-be-forgotten experience. The system had two cars, one at each end of the cable, so that as one ascended, the other car descended. At the half way point the cars passed each other on a pair of divergent tracks. At the top was the steam powered station that moved the cable over an enormous wheel. From the station it was only a short walk to the Catskill Mountain House and the superb view from the lawn in front and the rocks at the top of the cliff.

Soon it was time to go back to the cable station and board the car for the return trip to the base. Again the views were excellent, and perhaps this time we noticed the passage over the big trestle, where the track was on a high bridge over a deep ravine. After walking back to the picnic ground, we would eventually hear Mr. Plush's loud banging on a kettle announcing that it was time to go back to the train. On the return trip to Catskill the children tended to be much less noisy than on the way out, but it was always the close of a wonderful day (and probably a time of relief for the half dozen Sunday School teachers who had accompanied us and whose job it was to maintain order).

THE CROW TRIBE

I was never a member of the Crow Tribe. Shorty was, and Bill Murray, and Wendell van Orden and Frank Wilcoxon, who later achieved fame for his pioneer work in non-parametric statistics. Sam Hopkins was the youngest member, partly because he built the cabins and partly because his presence gave legitimacy to the use of Hopkins property. It all started when Sam decided to build a log cabin near a spring in the lower part of the valley east of The Ridge. Fairly big trees surrounded the spring.

I remember helping Sam build the log cabin, which turned out to be too small for a comfortable gathering. Soon it had an annex, a larger cabin built of boards, featuring a large stone fireplace, and equipped with a table, chairs and cooking utensils.

The Crow Tribe developed spontaneously, using the cabin complex for food and relaxation. It is alleged that some of Aunt Hattie's chickens were shot and cooked. Hopkins chickens were also said to have disappeared into the pot. Harry and I were tolerated chiefly to run errands, and Shorty's admonition to "skip" eventually was transformed to what became my local nickname, "Skibo," which I was careful not to take with me to college.

Most memorable were the late afternoons in front of the blazing fire. Often today when I am seated in front of a fire I have a mental picture of Frank Wilcoxon resting comfortably with his pipe held in place by a metal pin between two of his false teeth. The dog, whose ownership and name I do not recall, was comfortable too. There was much semi-grown-up talk and much plain loafing in a comfortable place, chief pastimes of the Crow Tribe. Sometimes the Crow Tribe operated in "Camp Rescue," a campfire site a hundred yards above the river shore with a magnificent view of the Hudson.

The Crow Tribe had no constitution or list of members, and I do not know how the name originated. It was a term of convenience covering a variable group of older boys who had found a haven in the woods for loafing, chatting, smoking and occasionally eating in front of a friendly fire.

THE DEMISE OF THE CATSKILL MOUNTAIN RAILROAD

The history of the Catskill Mountain Railroad starts with the centennial celebration of American independence in 1876. According to the story, there was a narrow gauge steam railroad circling the grounds of the exposition in Philadelphia. After the exposition closed, track and equipment were acquired for a much needed route for passengers and freight from Catskill to the growing resort areas of Greene County.

From New York to Catskill there was already good service by rail and steamer, with an additional rail line west of the river under construction. Somehow a route through Austin's Glen to Cairo and on to Palenville was financed and laid out, and a connection made via the Otis Elevated to the mountaintop. It provided an excellent alternative to horsedrawn transportation until the automobile appeared a few decades later. Then there was no way it could avoid bankruptcy.

As a much-interested 15-year-old spectator, I attended the auction of assets held on the steps of the Greene County courthouse in Catskill. James P. Phillips, president of the Catskill National Bank, had announced he wanted to buy the railroad and keep it running. He was present, but went across the street to his bank to get cash to back up his bid. When he returned the railroad had been sold to a New York bidder for junk, which was probably just as well for Mr. Phillips' fortune. Some time later a wrecking crew had a wreck of their own in Austin's Glen. A car was derailed and slid down the bank toward the stream. Raymond Taylor and I heard about it and hiked out to see for ourselves. The track had been cleared and a train consisting of an engine and two or three flat cars was about to leave for the end of the line to pick up a load of rails. We sought out the man in charge and asked if we might ride out and back. He pointed at the car down the embankment and said "yes," but at our own risk. Although the month was December, the weather was perfect and the ride was glorious. I had taken the same trip many times on Sunday School picnics, but this trip was a revelation. We could see all around! Familiar spots took on new meaning from the perspective of a rapidly-moving flat car.

When we reached the outskirts of Palenville we found that a few rails had already been shipped and more were ready to load, but Raymond and I decided that loading would take considerable time. We took off for a hike, we were already in Palenville Clove, a mile or so from the train, when we heard a whistle. We hurried back and found that the train had gone! It was beginning to get dark.

There was nothing to do but hike back ten miles or so to Catskill on the Palenville road. Unfortunately there was no traffic and no chance to solicit a ride. When we reached Catskill we turned up Allen Street towards Raymond's. There outdoors were both Mrs. Taylor and my mother who had been so worried that she had walked half a mile in the dark to see if Raymond's mother had any information. We were tired and contrite. I remember no reprimand for what had been defective judgment.

Many years later I saw Raymond from time to time at the annual meetings of the American Association for the Advancement of Science. He was a Ph.D. in biology with entomology as his specialty, and for a time taught at the university level; he gave up teaching in favor of an administrative position with the prestigious American Association for the Advancement of Science. One year, when I was serving as president of the Psychometric Society, I received an official communication from the AAAS, with the salutation "Dear Dr. DuBois" and signed, quite properly, "Raymond L. Taylor." Had it required an answer, I might have mentioned our earlier and closer association.

FOURTH OF JULY

Almost always the fourth of July for Harry and me followed the same pattern. Without restriction, we were allowed to buy small firecrackers, sparklers and torpedoes. We were also permitted to buy a few large firecrackers, a pin wheel or two, some Roman candles and three or four rockets. During the day we had wonderful fun in a sand box, firing small firecrackers from two iron cannon, four or five inches long, that seemed to have been made for the purpose, each having a hole in the barrel for the fuse. We always used brown, slow burning punk to ignite any type of fireworks. Its slightly pungent odor was pleasant.

In early evening, with adults present, we would set off our scanty supply of display pieces. At all times we were under strict admonitions to be exceedingly careful. We never had an accident. We had glimpses of fireworks set off by summer visitors across the road, and occasionally a glimpse of a distant rocket. Before they became illegal, it was fun to watch the hot air balloons go by. Four or five feet in height, they were made of colored strips of paper. A small burner provided both lift and illumination. Theoretically the fuel would be all consumed before the balloon landed, but this was not always the case and they were eventually banned as fire hazards. When they were common, the Pine Lot would often yield a burned out balloon or two on the morning of July 5.

One year, probably 1916, the Hopkins family asked whether they could set off their fireworks at the top of the Pine Lot. The idea was welcomed and the Browns and DuBoises assembled with the Hopkins to watch the display. The Hopkins brought over a wash basket filled with a fine assortment of fireworks as well as a guest, a German youth whose first name was Hans. All went well until Hans was invited to light and handle a Roman candle, which discharges balls of fire. Somehow a spark landed in the basket of fireworks. We scattered in several directions as the pieces were ignited and flames shot out. That ended our most memorable celebration.

MEMORIAL DAY WITH THE G.A.R.

Civil War veterans had high visibility and much political importance in the early part of the century. Although by 1915 the war had been over for fifty years, there were still a number of veterans banded together as the G.A.R., the Grand Army of the Republic. The Bagley brothers had a grandfather who had been a general and lived to an advanced age. One veteran who worked briefly at The Ridge told of bullets whistling close to him during a battle.

In the village cemetery there was a bronze statue of a Civil War soldier surrounded by a circle of graves, each with a headstone indicating military connection and a small flag at the foot. Fresh flowers and new flags were added on Memorial Day. There was always a parade. In early days the veterans marched, later they rode in automobiles, always with their campaign hats embellished with insignia and their large G.A.R. badges on their chests. The parade ended at the statue, where the brief ceremony concluded with the recitation of Lincoln's Gettysburg address by the high school senior who had won the annual James P. Phillips Speaking Contest. In my senior year Bill Thorpe made the presentation beautifully.

THEATERS IN CATSKILL

The Nelida Theater was opened, probably in the 1880's, with a performance of Joseph Jefferson in *Rip Van Winkle*. With respect to the theatre's name, one of the builders was said to have a Nelly for a wife, while the wife of the other was named Ida.

I remember a number of special occasions without being able to arrange them in chronological order: concerts by Sousa and his band and by the rival band of Arthur Pryor; a gala performance of three movies in a single evening; and the memorable *Birth of a Nation*, for which I had carefully saved fifty cents for a gallery seat. While the Nelida was showing movies regularly in what was called an opera house, the Irving Theater, built specifically as a movie house, opened a block or so up the street. It had a main floor and two balconies, the upper balcony commanding an admission price of five cents for matinees.

One New Year's Eve the Nelida was used for a party which was followed, after participants had left, with a fire that resulted in a total loss. I saw the ruins a day or two later—charred timbers in enormous snow banks, masses of ice formed from water from firemen's hoses. This left the Irving Theater with a movie monopoly. After a time Mr. Silberstein, owner and editor of the *Catskill Daily Mail*, claimed that Mr. Lansing of the Irving Theater was substituting poorer pictures for those which had been advertised. Finally Mr. Silberstein and others built the Community Theater on the Nelida site, designed for both stage productions and motion pictures. It opened with *The Quaker Girl*, which I think was my first musical comedy. Some years later the Irving Theater made way for a retail store.

The movies in the early days around 1912 were crude compared with modern films: silent with piano accompaniment (orchestra in the cities but not in Catskill); subtitles for dialogue and to provide orientation; no color; elaborate gesturing; simple plots; lots of Western scenery. One of the first actors I remember was a comic, John Bunny, who was soon banned from the screen because of improper conduct in his personal life. Of course we loved Charlie Chaplin comedies and the adventures of Douglas Fairbanks. We used to debate the relative merits of Mary Pickford and rivals, such as Mary Miles Minter. Of particular interest in Catskill was a local starlet who was a friend of Grace's, Anne Cornwall. She actually appeared in a couple of feature films which were warmly received in Catskill. After she married a director, she apparently disappeared from movie history.

Some stage stars were recruited for the films and I have vague recollections of seeing performances by Nazimova and Sarah Bernhardt. Until D.W. Griffith's *Birth of a Nation*, movies consisted of shorts. However, newsreels, comedies such as the early Chaplin pictures, and cartoons supplemented the features.

Mother saw enough motion pictures to be able to exercise informed judgment about what was suitable for her young sons. Almost always we attended matinees, frequently in the company of Pell Hopkins, whose parents found the DuBois children excellent escorts.

MILITARY TRAINING

Shortly before the end of World War I, New York State began a military training program for boys. I had two years of the program, one when I was below the compulsory age of 16, and the second when I was 16. After that the law was repealed.

We met once a week in the Armory on Bridge Street. The Armory was used primarily for the training of the National Guard, which was called to active duty in time of war and replaced with the Home Guard, volunteers not in active military service.

Captain Wilbur was in charge of our training. He was a chubby, pleasant fellow who was conscientious in running his program and adept at maintaining discipline without annoying his trainees. He wore a uniform; we did not. There was marching at first, then the manual of arms with the real rifles kept in locked cases at the armory, then bayonet drill. Once we went on a march of several miles in loose formation. It was all good exercise in company of youngsters of about the same age. Had the war continued we would have been partially trained recruits.

Some 25 years later, during World War II, my friend Edward Jones was commander of the Home Guard in Catskill. He was a captain and when I, in uniform as a major, appeared for a friendly visit, he said,

"Generally speaking, I don't like majors." His remark was based on his experience with higher ups from Albany.

HOBBIES

A wonderful aspect of growing up is that there seems to be time for everything, including hobbies. In Catskill I had three hobbies: stamp collecting, coin collecting and photography.

Shorty had been a stamp collector for years. He had two enormous albums with stamps scattered throughout. However, he lost interest before I started my collection with a more practical album. He gave me his entire accumulation. By mail I bought a couple of packages of 1,000 inexpensive stamps and spent hours mounting them. I took a trial subscription or two to *McKeel's Weekly Stamp News*. I sent for some "approvals," but I seldom spent more than a dime for a stamp.

I made more progress with United States stamps than with those from foreign countries, making an excursion to Hudson to visit with a Mr. Wendover Neefus, who advertised in *McKeel's Weekly*. He turned out to be a lawyer who sold stamps by mail from his office. Dad helped me with stamps that came his way in the store, and I found some good ones, with Aunt Hattie's permission, in Uncle Harvey's trunk after he died. My collection of United States stamps included specimens from all 19th century issues as well as being more or less complete for regular and commemorative stamps of the first quarter of the 20th century. Foreign revenue stamps were considered of no interest, but I developed a fair collection of U.S. revenues, aided by stamps from Dad's store and some documentary stamps sprinkled through Uncle Harvey's papers.

When I was in Lebanon, I used a variety of the picturesque local stamps on my letters home with strict instruction to save them for my return. I also accumulated complete unused sets, and always it has been my practice to save every interesting stamp arriving at my desk. Whenever I know of a relative with an interest in stamps I have some highly acceptable gifts. Present acquisitions are mostly plate blocks of American commemoratives, but I still have lots of philatelic paper stashed away.

Dad had a coin collection which he kept in a large round leather box. He was proud of a silver dollar issued during Maximilian's short reign as emperor of Mexico. Dad also had a number of mid-nineteenth century coins including at least one silver 20-cent piece.

I collected pennies, including a few old large-sized coins. I sought out dates and mint marks through about 1925, when I put all my coins in Dad's box and left for Lebanon.

I spent far more time and effort on photography. Again I profited from Shorty's example. He had used a box camera for some pictures around The Ridge and had done his own finishing. My Christmas present in 1917 was a folding Brownie, with a rapid rectilinear lens (whatever that was) and the "autographic feature," under patent rights acquired by Eastman Kodak. Instead of shielding the film with paper red on one side and black on the other, the black lining was replaced with a sort of carbon paper. After each exposure one could open a special slot on the camera, write in the space with a stylus, expose the opening for a few seconds and expect to see the inscription attached to the negative when the roll was developed. I had some success with the feature, but pressure on the stylus and subsequent exposure were hard to get just right. Another difficulty was that the first part of the inscription tended to come out differently than the latter part. Apparently others encountered similar troubles, since Kodak abandoned the idea after a few years. But for a time the "autographic feature" was at the forefront of amateur photographic technology.

Dad stocked tubes of tiny sized blue print paper in his store in Athens, and I used some in my first essays into printing from negatives. It was a very simple process: in subdued daylight the paper was put behind the negative in a frame, then exposure to sunlight until inspection showed uniform hue, then fixing in a bath of plain water. Soon, however, I graduated to a makeshift darkroom in the bathroom with trays of chemicals and a red safelight. I learned how to develop negatives as well as how to make prints and dry them on a sheet suspended flat.

THE SUMMIT HILL HOUSE FIRE

Half a mile west of The Ridge was the Summit Hill House which catered to summer visitors from the New York area. It was here that Mary Pell, a New York socialite, was staying when she met Sam Hopkins.

One summer day Shorty rushed into house shouting, "The Summit Hill House is on fire!" And sure enough it was: Through the trees we could see billowing smoke as well as tongues of flames. Harry and I were not permitted to leave the premises but Shorty went over for a closer look. This was the end of the Summit Hill House—it was never rebuilt.

Dad regarded this particular fire, which occurred in mid-summer, as legitimate. He said that boarding house fires generally occurred at the end of the season.

HALLEY'S COMET

I have experienced two visitations by Halley's comet, in 1910 and again in 1986. The first was spectacular and memorable—the second only on TV and forgettable except for commercially induced enthusiasm: cruises, telescope sales and books.

In 1910 I remember Mother's Aunt Kate in Athens talking about the coming of the comet. She was old enough to remember its previous visit. In the newspapers it was reported that some individuals thought that the world was coming to an end and there was a suicide or two. In fact it was in that context that I learned the word suicide. At The Ridge all was serene but all of us hoped to see the visitor.

Shorty showed me the comet. He woke me up, took me out on the lawn and pointed west, over the mountains. He didn't need to point. There was Halley's comet, a brilliant object in the fading sunset. The head was down, close to the mountains, and the luminous tail fanned out as it reached heaven-ward. Its apparent length was several times the apparent height of the mountains—and it looked much like its pictures in the newspapers. I remember my sister Grace saying to me, "If you live to be as old as Granddaddy, you'll see Halley's comet again." Well, we were both alive in 1986, but in that year Halley's comet was a non-event except for astronomers and purveyors of cruises and telescopes.

When Vernon Helming and I were in Normandy in 1925 we noted Halley's comet on the Bayeux tapestry that depicts events of the conquest of England by William the Conqueror in 1066. The 1910 appearance seems to have been the eleventh subsequent visit.

At the age of 16 Shorty developed a special interest in comets as evidenced by his use of newspaper accounts to locate Brook's comet, visible later that summer. He pointed it out to me: visible to the naked eye and almost directly overhead. It looked like a star, but with a long, thin tail stretching toward the east. It was not nearly as spectacular as Halley's comet but still an event.

ICE HOUSES

For years the ice houses along the Hudson and on Catskill Creek played an important role in the local economy. They were used to store ice that was harvested like a crop and shipped by barge during the summer for use in New York City. They were huge box-like structures built with double wooden walls to keep cold in and heat out. The ice was packed in sawdust.

The introduction of artificial ice caused great concern to the ice industry, as evidenced by an advertising campaign which praised the non-existent virtues of "natural ice" over the kind made by machine. Ice harvested from the river contained various impurities and perhaps germs and the ultimate demise of natural ice was in the public interest.

Work with the ice harvest provided winter work to many men in the Catskill area and prosperity to proprietors of the facilities, such as Minot Seaman, father of friends of ours and owner of a couple of ice houses. His large home on a bluff overlooking the river and with a magnificent view exuded wealth. (Years later the estate was purchased by Mike Tyson, heavyweight champion.)

The most dangerous assignment was a job analogous to a first step in mining: staking out claims. This was done as soon as the ice was thick enough to support a man. There was sufficient movement by the tide and the flow of water so that cracks in the ice could develop before it was thick enough to harvest. The ideal ice was clear but sometimes it was harvested with a thin covering of snow.

Some workers reported to an ice house when they were reasonably confident that the harvest would begin. Others would wait until they heard a siren signaling the need for men. Qualified individuals who reported at an office shack were assigned work under the foreman for a particular job: sawing ice to a specified size with a huge saw, pushing blocks of ice with poles along a canal, cutting blocks apart as they passed under a bridge, loading the ice on an elevator or distributing it in the ice house. One cold day I watched an enormous busy scene that might have been painted by Grandma Moses.

Workers were paid well and in cash. A silver dollar which Shorty brought home one evening looked so big to me that I thought it was a $5 piece!

In seasons other than winter an ice house dock and the channel leading to it were very convenient way stations for the tiny steamers that called at Catskill, Hudson and Athens. And in summer a dock was a fine place for swimming after one had learned the fundamentals and was ready to try diving from a few feet above the water. There was always a ladder to climb up or down. In late summer the interior of an ice house would be a huge darkish void with a few rays of sunlight reaching the sawdust on the floor. Our interest was always outside.

As the industry died there was attempt to devise alternate uses for the old buildings, such as raising mushrooms. The ice houses along both sides of the river now have been pulled down but somewhere along one of the creeks one survives as a place to grow mushrooms. When plans developed to dredge the river to permit ocean going traffic to Albany and to use ice breakers to keep the channel open all through the winter, there was no ice industry left to oppose the development. And now one can no longer walk on the ice to cross the river between Athens and Hudson or between Catskill Point and Greendale as I did more than once.

ENTERING THE ADULT WORLD

BARBER SHOPS

W HEN a boy is growing up, a barber shop is a place where, after the very early years, he goes alone and becomes the center of attention while the barber is cutting his hair. While waiting his turn he may have almost grown-up contacts with other customers.

My earliest recollections of barbers are from Newburgh, where the shops were open Sunday mornings for men who wanted a shave before church. No hair cutting on Sundays! I probably had earlier involvement, but the occasion I remember most clearly came shortly after my fourth birthday when a barber was instructed to cut off my Dutch bob. My verbal resistance was ineffective.

I don't remember any haircuts at home so Mother probably took me to the barber until I was old enough to go to Amon Schmidt's shop on Main Street all by myself. His second floor room was simple and clean with one barber's chair in front of the mirror and several chairs for waiting customers. He was kindly but tolerated no nonsense. The price was $.20—no tip! He made apologies when he raised his price to a quarter.

Schmidt had a bicycle with a motor attachment on which he had a bad spill and was away from work for a while. Thereafter he had bad things to say about attachments used to motorize bicycles. Such attachments eventually went out of production, probably because of their poor safety record.

The big barber shop in Catskill was Klein's with several barbers. In a backroom barbers at leisure played cards. Tips were expected and received. I think I stayed with Amon Schmidt as long as he was in business but eventually I patronized Klein's—tip and the flavor of gambling notwithstanding.

THE GROCERY TRUCK THAT HIT ME

With one of the "boarders" at Kerr's I was sitting on a fence protecting a culvert on the highway in front of The Ridge when a large flatbed grocery truck coming from the north swerved toward us, apparently to give us a scare. It came too close and hit me just below the knee. The truck went on, but slowed down. We went across the road and started up the hill, but when my companion saw blood flowing down my leg, he shouted at the driver with a New York oath.

The driver came back. I climbed on the truck and by the time we reached the village there was a pool of blood beside me. Dr. Honeyford took a number of stitches, saying that an artery had been severed. One of the Smith brothers who owned the grocery came to see me while I was still in the doctor's office.

An account in the paper, apparently given by Jesse Warrington, the driver, stated that the boys were running after the truck, an obvious misstatement. Dr. Honeyford treated the injury until it was fully healed, with the bill paid by the Smiths. In modern times they would have been sued! And Dr. Honeyford's prediction that I would have the scar as long as I lived has been true for more than seven decades.

THE COURT HOUSE

You might say that the Greene County Courthouse is next to the Dutch Reformed Church. Or vice versa. For me the church was more familiar but as time went on I became familiar with the courthouse also. Raymond Taylor showed me its chief use for a youngster—toilets were clean and accessible.

After Theodore Roosevelt lost his bid for the Presidency in 1912, he kept his Bull Moose party alive. In 1914 he spoke on the courthouse steps on behalf of a Mr. Davenport, who was running for governor on the Bull Moose or Progressive ticket. Students were permitted to leave high school for the happening. We reached the courthouse just as proceedings were closing, and Mr. Roosevelt was already in the back seat of an automobile. Among us Raymond Taylor was the boldest. He walked up to the car, put out his hand and said, "Shake hands, Teddy." Teddy did! Then there were a number of youngsters who lined up to follow Raymond. The handshake that Mr. Roosevelt gave me was the quickest I have ever experienced but an event lasting less than a second can be remembered for years.

In high school we were encouraged to attend trials at the courthouse. The most memorable trial I attended involved a young man accused of shooting another. An expert witness demonstrated some of the items of a test which had been developed by a French psychologist, Alfred Binet. The witness defined a moron in terms of measured mental ability in relation to age and identified the accused as a moron. The verdict in the case took into account the testimony of the expert, who was probably H. H. Goddard of the Vineland Training School in New Jersey, the psychologist who translated the Binet tests into English. In college I was to hear more about Binet and his tests and in graduate school I was to develop considerable expertise in psychological measurement.

NEWSPAPER WORK

My first town job was night work at *The Recorder*, one of the three weekly newspapers in Catskill. I inherited the job from Edward Jones who for some reason wanted to give it up. Every Thursday evening beginning about eight o'clock, I operated the addressing machine, beginning with the labels for bundles and then stamping the individual copies for places with a single subscriber. I soon learned the names of dozens of villages and tiny settlements where *The Recorder* had loyal readers: Coeymans, Oak Hill, Ravena, Prattsville, Tannersville, Medusa, Cornwallville, South Durham.

When the job was done, usually about midnight, the elder Mr. Hall (father of the scoutmaster), who was owner, editor and publisher, would look at his watch and pay for the night's work. Neither Edward nor I ever discovered his formula but took whatever was offered, usually in the $1.75 to $2.25 range.

My second newspaper job was in the summer of 1921 with *The Catskill Examiner*, a competitor of *The Recorder* but not its equal in circulation or importance. It was managed by Alan Craigie, son of the owner, who brought to the paper professional experience in New York and a gift for teaching a novice the basics of reporting. Accepted practices included: no editorial comment, all individuals mentioned should have first name or two initials; Miss or Mrs. was to be used but no Mr., except later in the story when it was used with only the last name; careful attention to grammar and spelling. Each full story was to be told three times: in the headline, in the lead paragraph and then in the body of the article. My salary was $10 a week and in the fall I used the $100 in the bills with which I was paid to cover initial college expenses.

My primary job was writing, using the hunt-and-peck system common with the newspaper reporters of the day, including Alan Craigie. The "personals," items about individuals, were 95% paraphrased from *The Daily Mail* which had Margarite Kaiser going up and down Main Street full time collecting news about out-of-town trips, such as going on business to Albany 35 miles away, visitors in town, celebrations and hospitalizations.

Occasionally Mr. Craigie would give me a real assignment such as covering the funeral of Judge Chase or the wedding of well known individuals such as the occasion when my classmate, Gertrude Morrison, and Harry Joseph, a local clothier, were married. After the ceremony I called on Gertrude's mother, who gave me all the details—clergyman, guests, dresses, menu—and I produced what I considered a fine article.

At *The Examiner* the staff included a linotype operator and a printer but I was the only reporter. When necessary Alan could handle any job. Hours were long and employment was for six days a week. The only time I was released from the schedule was after working two or three times all Friday night to get the paper out by Saturday morning. I was then told to stay home Saturday to recuperate.

The first time that happened I didn't communicate with Mother since we had no telephone. When I appeared at 5 or 6 o'clock A.M., she had to be reassured that my absence was strictly in line of business.

On Saturdays I collected my salary twice. With a handful of bills I would call on people whose subscriptions were in arrears or whose subscriptions were about to expire. A goodly proportion paid promptly but every once in a while I was told to "cancel the subscription." This I always reported to Mr. Craigie but characteristically he continued the name on the subscription list and in more than one case I went through the same routine the following year. I generally collected enough cash so that Alan could meet the weekly payroll, including my $10.

After my freshman year at college I worked another summer on *The Examiner*, this time for $12 a week. The following summer I asked for $20 a week. Mr. Craigie said I was well worth it, but that he could not pay that much, so my next newspaper job was on *The Schenectady Gazette*.

EPIDEMICS

In the fall of 1918 came the flu epidemic, "Spanish influenza," which wrought havoc in Europe and the United States. It caused many deaths in Catskill. I got it early. Shorty was in France, Grace in New York, Dad in Newburgh. I believe neither Mother or Harry had it. I was quite sick but Mother provided loving care. After a time the fever passed and it was a wonderful day when I was strong enough to take a walk in the woods.

We heard about catastrophic events in town, including deaths of friends and acquaintances. The YMCA was turned into a temporary hospital and some of the Boy Scouts we knew, including George Bagley, earned credit toward a merit badge by working there. It was a cause for rejoicing when the plague ceased.

When I was a youngster, individuals with faces covered with small pox scars were frequently seen on the streets. My first experience in a smallpox epidemic was in Newburgh. Mother and Dad saw that we were all vaccinated. Mine didn't take. Since Grace was a girl her vaccination was not on her upper left arm but in a place where the scar presumably would not show, a bit above the knee. I believe her vaccination was successful.

The next scare was in Catskill. Again I was vaccinated, this time with success. However, in playing with Edward Jones I scraped both legs just below the knee with the result that the vaccination "took" in three places, on the arm and on both legs.

In Schenectady there was another round of small pox and one of my fraternity brothers, Horace Van Voast, was one of the victims. I was in Catskill when he became ill and returned to the campus to find the fraternity house quarantined. Somehow it was decided that, as I probably had been exposed, I should join my quarantined brethren, which prevented scheduled participation in the preparation of the college yearbook. When a doctor came to the house to check each one of us for small pox symptoms he was astonished by John Davis' high fever but John had merely touched a radiator with the thermometer when the doctor wasn't looking. "Hoddy" Van Voast was the only one of us who actually developed small pox, but he recovered to live to be well over eighty.

When I was in Beirut in the late 1920's, I was in another small pox scare. A visitor from a country to the south—Egypt, I think—developed the disease and once more I was vaccinated, with immune reaction. And this final scare did not last long.

A FEW TRAGIC INCIDENTS

Murders and other tragic events seemed rare in Catskill and the county surrounding, perhaps because of the sparse population, but from time to time there were violent happenings. I remember the case of Worthy Tolley, a farmer who lived a few miles north of Catskill and who was a relative of Aunt Ella's husband. He was working in his orchard when a neighbor boy taunted him by saying he had a letter from Worthy's son, who had run away. When the boy refused to give any further information, Worthy went inside his house and brought out a shotgun with which he finally shot the boy. Brought to trial in Catskill, he was convicted of first degree murder, sentenced to death and electrocuted at Sing Sing Prison. I do not know what appeals were made, but the case moved very fast. As a farmer without much money he did not hire an expensive lawyer, the kind that sometimes is successful in reducing the initial charge or, after a conviction, can delay or even circumvent the penalty.

Aunt Hattie visited Worthy while he was in jail in Catskill and later told of the happening. When she approached his cell, he put out his hand and said, "How do you do, Mrs. Brown?" Aunt Hattie took his hand and said, "Why did you do it, Worthy?" His answer was not reported, but when Aunt Hattie returned home she said, "I never thought I would shake hands with a murderer!"

One time in Catskill a very popular young physician pricked his hand through his rubber glove during an operation. A colleague offered appropriate treatment. He refused, saying the matter was of no consequence. But it was of consequence: infection developed and in a short time the young physician was dead.

Several young men in an automobile thought they could beat a West Shore train over a crossing. They too lost their lives.

Ruth Hammer, a classmate of mine in one of the lower grades, was picking wildflowers with a friend when a man approached them. They tried to run away, but were shot dead. He was apparently some sort of a mental case, for when his quarters at Hansen's greenhouse were searched a confession was found of a similar incident but which actually had not occurred. On my way to school I always passed the home of Ruth's parents, often remembering the tragedy.

Tragic events involving strangers from New York resulted in big headlines in the *Catskill Daily Mail*. I recall two such incidents, one of which happened when I was a reporter for *The Examiner*. A young woman gave birth in a public restroom and the baby was found dead. While the *Mail* called it a case of infanticide, I remember the district attorney telling me that there is no such crime. If criminal action is involved in causing the death of any human being, the appropriate charge is murder. As I remember, the case ended quietly. In the second incident a girl's body was found floating in a creek in a remote area— eventually evaluated as suicide.

Many years later a notorious gangster, Legs Diamond, made his headquarters in Greene County, indicating that there was some northward movement of criminals operating in New York City, but during my years in Catskill crime reported in the local press consisted of isolated incidents. I do not know the crime rate as compared with that of urban centers, but the impression was that it was much, much lower.

One incident involved Legs Diamond's name. When I was finishing my graduate studies I was eligible to be a "Certified Psychologist," but, before being filed, my papers had to be endorsed by a judge of a court of record. I was living in New York, where the papers were to be deposited, but there I knew no qualified judge; but I knew that Judge Thorpe, father of a classmate, would remember me. Accordingly, I made a trip to Catskill where he willingly signed my papers. When I took my papers to the New York City Hall, the clerk looked at them and said, "Judge Thorpe! He signed Legs Diamond's pistol permit, didn't he?" He had, indeed — but unknowingly he had been tricked.

READING

About the time I finished seventh grade my reading habits changed. Membership in the Boy Scouts resulted in subscribing to *Boys' Life*, with stories of camping and adventure. *The Youth's Companion* came every week, and once a year one of Mother's friends brought us her accumulation of *St. Nicholas* magazine. All three were completely wholesome and I read them avidly. While we never took them home, Pell Hopkins made available the volumes of *The Book of Knowledge*, an encyclopedia for young people, which I found exceedingly informative. At home our daily paper was the *Knickerbocker Press*, published in Albany, which kept us abreast of events at home and abroad.

Somewhere I came across a statement that if one were to read three chapters in the Bible every weekday and ten chapters each Sunday, one could read it all in a year. I decided to try the plan. I kept track of my daily stint and finished the reading on schedule, including all the genealogies and enumerations. I even started a second reading, but this carried over to college days when the press of activities led me to discontinue the effort. In a parallel endeavor I was aided by a list of 100 great novels printed on a small piece of yellow paper, origin not identified. It led me to read some wonderful books: *Romola, Mill on the Floss, John Halifax, Gentleman, Lorna Doone, Cranford, Pride and Prejudice*, and many others—about half of the list.

I also ventured into oriental literature with FitzGerald's translation of the *Rubaiyat*, which I liked to the point of memorizing some of the quatrains, and the *Mahabharata*, which was difficult sledding, and the *Ramayana*, which was more understandable. Some of this reading of the classics continued into college days; I don't know how I read so much and still was valedictorian in high school and graduated with honors in college. One high school habit was useful: being seated at my desk at six o'clock in the morning and studying for more than an hour before breakfast.

THE EIGHTH GRADE

In the Catskill school system the eighth grade differed from prior grades. Here seventh grade graduates of the Irving School on the east side of Catskill Creek and the Grandview School on the west side were grouped together. For the first and only time, pupils were segregated by sex. Ella Delamater taught the girls, Henry Thomas the boys. The two rooms were on different sides of the first floor of the high school building. For reasons the students could never divine, Miss Delamater and Mr. Thomas absented themselves from their classrooms again and again for short conferences in neutral territory.

Eighth grade was supposed to be transitional between grade school and high school, but the only new features were location, segregation of boys and girls, and an influx of new friends. There were no electives, no study hall between classes, no change of teachers for different subjects.

Mr. Thomas was the only male teacher in either the grade or high school. He was slight in build, nearing retirement and somewhat timid in manner. His favorite hymn was "It's Christmas Day on the Ocean," which he played on a tiny organ. When it came time to go home he would call us to order and dismiss us one by one, usually beginning with "Floyd Bump may pass." For some reason or other Mr. Thomas seemed to be a bit afraid of Floyd.

MISS ROOT

Mabel V. Root was a lifelong friend of my mother's. They had been schoolmates and their intimacy resumed as soon as the DuBois family moved to Catskill. After high school she majored in classical languages at Cornell University and for many years taught Latin officially and the cultural life unofficially in Catskill High School. Her skills and breadth of interests would have permitted a career at the university level, but family concerns required her presence in Catskill. She had three siblings, all of whom at maturity became blind with detached retina, incurable in those days. Mrs. Root, the mother, was a knowledgeable and strong-minded widow who received a few permanent paying guests in her home, notably Dr. Hazzard, the pastor of the Presbyterian Church, who was said to have read all the books in the Catskill Public Library. Edith, the sister with a buoyant personality, was the family cook, blindness notwithstanding. Ed, the brother, was able to get around the vicinity to tend furnaces. The other sister, Hattie, was amiable but somewhat reclusive.

Everything at the Root home was in good taste: the antique furniture, the oriental rugs, the pictures on the wall, the extensive book collection. There was a great deal of reading aloud and Mabel, as the eyes of her siblings, developed wonderful skills in verbal description. One day Mother and I were invited to go for a drive with Miss Root and her sister Edith. While Edith was directly sensitive only to sounds, breezes, temperature and woodsy odors, her experience was nearly complete, thanks to the vivid descriptions that came almost continuously from Mabel. A year or so before World War I, Miss Root took the trip of a lifetime for a Latin teacher, a visit to classical sites in Italy and Greece. When she returned she brought Mother a tinted print of one of the portals of St. Marks Cathedral in Venice, which thereafter hung in the DuBois parlor. And at the age of nine or ten I listened with interest to the accounts of her travels she gave Mother.

LATIN AT CATSKILL HIGH SCHOOL

Grace and possibly Shorty studied Latin with Miss Root in high school. Grace took all four years: first year, Caesar, Cicero and Virgil, and distinguished herself by winning the Latin Prize. It was taken for granted that Latin would be one of my high school electives and year after year I signed up.

Miss Root decorated her classroom with photographs of classical sculptures. There were two models executed in modeling clay, the Colosseum and the Roman Forum, made by students in earlier years. They were sufficiently realistic to be a good introduction to the actual scenes a few years later.

Aided by Miss Root's patience and persistence, the first year class learned some Latin: vocabulary, conjugations and declensions, and then we read *The Argonauts,* a tale in synthetic Latin of Jason's quest for the Golden Fleece. After Caesar's Gallic War in the sophomore year, third year Cicero was more fun. Raymond Taylor translated part of the Oration against Catiline into current slang, for example, calling Catiline a "rotten egg." Miss Root liked that. My copy of Virgil's first six books of *The Aeneid* has markings through to the end of the text on page 187, dated June 9,1921, which indicates sizable stints of reading throughout the year.

During an illness in my third year I produced the dummy of a Latin class publication which I called "The Mud Puddle." The class liked the idea of a monthly magazine but at Raymond Taylor's suggestion it was rechristened "The Spotlight." I claimed to be too busy to be editor, but Mary Vedder was willing to handle the job, which she did with distinction. I was "mimeograph editor," which means that once a month I cranked out the copies. Miss Weir, the business teacher, showed me how to keep the machine properly inked, with the result that in graduate school I made a reputation for myself for the quality of my mimeographing. The publication continued through our two remaining years in high school and for at least one year thereafter.

From time to time Miss Root took her students on geology walks in Austin's Glen, but flowers, plants, trees and skyscapes were observed as well as rocks. She seemed to notice everything of interest.

Twice members of our class were invited to a weekend house party at Stillwinkle, a cabin on a ledge of the Catskills up above Palenville. Its name reflects the fanciful notion that it was the place where the beverage was prepared that put Rip Van Winkle to sleep for twenty years. The owner of the cabin, Miss Emily Becker, village librarian, had filled it with books. Once Miss Root told her it lacked a French dictionary, but on her next visit the cabin had acquired one. For the weekend we all contributed food—my mother sent a basket of little cakes—and behavior was decorous. There were meals in the open air and hikes up the mountain to higher elevations. And there were whip-poor-wills calling incessantly in the moonlight.

OTHER TEACHERS IN CATSKILL HIGH SCHOOL

In the early 1920's Catskill High School had a fine complement of teachers, all competent women. Miss Weir taught typing and engineering drawing. I tried her drawing class for a few meetings. I liked it, but it was too much of an overload and I withdrew. Raymond Taylor took typing and became proficient but at a later time I contented myself with the two-finger system prevalent at *The Examiner*.

Miss Wallace taught languages. Unfortunately, during World War I the teaching of German was discontinued in many schools. To ringing applause our school superintendent, Mr. Hocmer, declared "the language of the Germans is not fit to study." With misguided patriotism, Edward Jones and I and a number of others elected Spanish as our modern foreign language. I got along in it but a quirk in the Union College rules required me to continue it in my freshman year at college. I made up for my mistake by taking a fine course in French in my sophomore year and by intensive tutoring in French when I was teaching at the American University of Beirut.

In addition to Miss Root, C.H.S. had two outstanding teachers. Miss Jackson was highly regarded as an administrator and as an English teacher. I had no special contact with her as a principal, but her presentation of *As You Like It* made the play memorable and vivid. When I read the same play in college, there seemed nothing new to learn. Miss Jackson resigned to accept a better position and was succeeded as principal by Miss Bronson. Quite properly in my senior year she vetoed me for the "good boy" prize on the grounds that I was often late and that once I had left the school without permission for a quick trip to Main Street. Virgil Baurheit deserved and received the prize.

The other extraordinary teacher was Miss Gardner who taught history and geometry. As with Miss Root, family reasons kept her in Catskill. All the courses I took with her were profitable but the best was History B. This was modern European history which became a fine background for European travel and many hours of reading on my own on the French revolution, the nineteenth and twentieth century in Europe, the partitions of Poland, the unifications of Germany and of Italy, and the development and the early stages of the decline of the colonial empires. Miss Gardner had the reputation of being strict but for decades I have been grateful for her effectiveness as a teacher.

I became something of a math shark in high school but I was good enough in other subjects so that academically I was first in a graduating class of twenty-eight.

L'ENVOI

In the spring of 1921 there was no question about my entering college, only where. Raymond Taylor, who was two years older than I, had graduated in 1920 after only three years in high school and also won a competitive scholarship for Cornell. With my "90-Count Diploma," representing five years work taken in four years, and my high grades, my chances of winning a similar award were excellent, but my parents thought Cornell too large. Rutgers offered a scholarship to match my New York State grant (one of four awarded in each Assembly district), but Dad had unpleasant memories of Rutgers Prep and vetoed the possibility. Shorty had been at Union both before and after his two years of wartime Army service, and Dad thought Union had many advantages: It was relatively small, it had an excellent reputation, and it was only fifty miles from home. When I applied, acceptance was immediate.

Shortly after Labor Day in 1921 a taxi came to the Ridge to take me to the ferry to Greendale where I took the train for Schenectady. I knew no one on the campus, but Shorty had arranged for some of his Psi Upsilon brothers to meet me at the station. A new chapter had begun. Boyhood was over.

POSTSCRIPT

HAPPILY there have been a number of subsequent chapters, the first of which comprised the four years at Union: a year in the dormitory followed by three years in a fraternity house. A number of campus activities including debating, the editorship of the undergraduate newspaper and participation in student government; and with graduation following specialization in languages. Then three fabulous years as an instructor in English at the American University of Beirut, which included contacts with students of diverse nationalities and backgrounds: Lebanese, Egyptians, Iraqis, Iranians, Greeks, Sunni and Shiite Moslems, Jews, and members of various Christian sects. Extensive travel in Europe and the Middle East (particularly to archeological sites) and a return to the United States by way of Damascus, Baghdad, Teheran, Moscow, the Trans-Siberian Railway, Manchuria, Peiping, Kyoto, the summit of Fuji, Tokyo and the Canadian Rockies.

The next chapter transpired in New York City, with International House providing the social environment and Columbia University the work situation: graduate studies leading to a Ph.D. in psychology, teaching and research at Columbia and an internship at Psychiatric Institute.

Two years at the Southern Branch of the University of Idaho at Pocatello involved an abrupt change of scene from New York streets to mountains with clear air, sagebrush and rattlesnakes. A heavy teaching load did not preclude fine contacts with faculty members from all departments, possible in a small school. However, I welcomed an invitation to move to a more advanced institution, the University of New Mexico in Albuquerque.

The New Mexico chapter included teaching advanced courses in psychology, directing graduate research, conducting student guidance and an extraordinary event: meeting and marrying Margaret Eloise Barclay, with whom I continue to share a long succession of happy years. Some extra curricular work as test technician and eventually supervisor of the New Mexico Merit System facilitated the purchase of our first home.

Just before we left New Mexico came four years in the Army Air Forces as an aviation psychologist. Our little family, which now included our daughter Margo, lived in San Antonio, St. Louis and Fort Worth as I—first as Captain, then Major and Lieutenant Colonel—worked on research projects involving the selection of pilots and other aviation specialists. A particularly stimulating experience was helping to introduce psychological selection tests in the air arm of the Free French during four months in wartime Algeria and Morocco.

A very long chapter involved a professorship at Washington University in St.Louis: teaching increasingly centered around quantitative methods in psychology; a wide range of consulting activities at different levels of government and in private industry; authorship of books and scientific papers; and directing and participating in professional conferences. Summer assignments involved family travel to Florida, California, England, Belgium, Italy and Egypt, as well as much travel without specific professional motivation.

Teaching continued until 1974. Since then there has been a pleasant mix of reading, writing and domestic duties: consulting in Memphis and St.Louis; trips to California to visit with our daughter and her family; and excursions to various European destinations, including France, Italy, Greece and what was then the Soviet Union. It has been a wonderful cup to sip—and Margaret Eloise and I are grateful!

THE DuBOIS LINE IN CATSKILL

Louis DuBois (1626-1696), son of Crétien DuBois of Wicres, France. Emigrated to America in 1660. Leader of Huguenots who founded New Paltz, N.Y.

Solomon DuBois (1669-1759), son of Louis. Purchased large tract of land at Catskill.

Benjamin DuBois (1697-1767), son of Solomon. Settled at Catskill in 1720 on land from his father. Bought additional land. In 1740 built the stone house across the creek from Catskill Point which became "ancestral home."

Isaac DuBois (1731-1795), son of Benjamin. An officer in the militia during the American Revolution. Inherited a large farm from his father, including the stone house in which he lived for 35 years.

Joel DuBois (1762-1844), son of Isaac. Served in the Revolution under his uncle, Lt. Col. Cornelius DuBois (1727-1803), Isaac's brother. Joel married Annatje DuBois (1769-1846), daughter of Cornelius. He was a farmer in Orange County, New York, later in Catskill.

Isaac J. DuBois (1789-1858), son of Joel and Annatje. Farmer in Kiskatom, town of Catskill.

Anson DuBois (1821-1905), son of Isaac J. DuBois. Grew up on his father's farm in the town of Catskill. As a minister of the Dutch Reformed Church he lived in various places but retained property in Kiskatom.

Henry R. DuBois (1868-1942), son of Anson. As a young man he spent some time in Kiskatom. A pharmacist, his base of operations beginning in 1908 was The Ridge in Catskill, to which he retired in 1924.

Henry R. DuBois, Jr. (b.1905), son of Henry. Grew up at The Ridge in Catskill (along with his brothers, Albert and Philip, and his sister Grace). He returned to Catskill as a banker in 1944, renovating and modernizing his home at The Ridge.

Henry R. DuBois, III (b.1945), son of Henry Jr. Grew up at The Ridge along with siblings David, Joan and Marjorie. A chemist. Current resident of The Ridge.

Joel DuBois (b.1974), son of Henry III. He and his sister, Alison Elizabeth, are the third generation of children at The Ridge. They are members of the ninth generation of DuBoises in Catskill and the eleventh generation in America.